·SCENES FROM AMERICAN CHURCH HISTORY·

FAITH
OF OUR
fathers

edited by
MARK SIDWELL

BJU PRESS
Greenville, South Carolina

Library of Congress Cataloging-in-Publication Data

Faith of our fathers : scenes from American church history / edited by Mark Sidwell

    Includes bibliographical references and index.
    ISBN 0-89084-602-2
    1. United States—Church history. 2. Christian biography—United States.
    3. Clergy—United States—Biography.   4. Protestant churches—United
    States—History.   I. Sidwell, Mark, 1958-
    BR515.F35   1991
    277.3—dc20   91-35667
                              CIP

NOTE:
The fact that materials produced by other publishers are referred to in this volume does not constitute an endorsement by Bob Jones University Press of the content or theological position of materials produced by such publishers. The position of Bob Jones University Press, and the University itself, is well known. Any references and ancillary materials are listed as an aid to the reader and in an attempt to maintain the accepted academic standards of the publishing industry.

Faith of Our Fathers: Scenes from American Church History
Edited by Mark Sidwell

Cover photograph by PhotoDisc, Inc.

Cover design by Seth Jaworski

ISBN 0-89084-602-2

15 14 13 12 11 10 9 8 7 6 5 4

Table of Contents

Introduction

In his brief sketch of the Great Awakening, *A Faithful Narrative of the Surprising Work of God,* Jonathan Edwards wrote, "'And whatever the circumstances and means have been, and though we are so unworthy, yet so hath it pleased God to work! And we are evidently a people blessed of the Lord! And here, in this corner of the world, God dwells and manifests his glory.''

By "this corner of the world," Edwards probably meant the small section of Massachusetts in which he lived. Yet his words are an appropriate description of America's history. We are indeed "a people blessed of the Lord," and we can indeed see that God has manifested His glory in this land. Although some Christians may have gone to extremes in trying to present the United States as the new "chosen nation" in the plans of God, it is certainly undeniable that America has a rich heritage of Christian faith—a heritage of which believers should be aware.

This collection is an attempt to expose Christians to that heritage and to provide some of the depth often missing in surveys of American church history. Although a useful tool for studying church history, the survey has its limitations. Often, for example, an author must omit illuminating detail because of the constraints of book size and the sheer breadth of the subject. If American church history may be likened to a broad, deep stream, then this work takes soundings of the depths at certain strategic points. A survey, by contrast, attempts to encompass the whole stream but rarely dips below the surface.

The present book arose in response to a perceived need in Christian circles—particularly for school teachers, pastors, and laymen. History teachers realize that a strict teaching of facts without illustration is the surest way to put a class to sleep. A collection such as this provides some of the stories and anecdotes that can enliven United States history. In particular, the articles collected here provide material that can awaken the student to the richness of America's Christian heritage.

For pastors and those who give devotionals, the need for illustrations is a constant problem. Although church history is an abundant source of illustrative material, surveys normally lack detail and books of illustrations often either sound contrived or are inaccurate. By reading these articles, the Christian is able not only to draw upon church history for illustrations but also to understand the illustrations in context and therefore be able to present them accurately.

The format of the book is designed to provide at least some overview of American church history and to underscore the principle-oriented thrust of the articles. The book divides into three sections—the first, on the Colonial Era (1607-1776), stressing in particular the founding of Christianity in America and the impact of the Great Awakening, the first of America's great revivals. The second section is on the Early National Era (1776-1865), discussing the Second Great Awakening and outlining the outstanding contributions that leading Christians made toward the growth of the young nation. The third section is on the Modern Era (1865 to the present). Here the book focuses on the outstanding men and women who typify movements in Christianity since the Civil War, notably evangelism and fundamentalism. An introduction to each section summarizes the chronology and main themes of the respective era.

Each article focuses on one person or topic. The majority of the articles are biographical, discussing individuals who are of great importance to history. Some of these people are well known (Roger Williams, Jonathan Edwards, D. L. Moody, Billy Sunday), while others are less familiar (Robert Hunt, Asahel Nettleton, John Chavis, Ford Porter). All of them, however, made important contributions. The book does not use biography exclusively, though. Articles on topics such as the Pilgrims, camp meetings, and circuit riders are also included. The brief paragraph that introduces each article discusses the place of the subject in church history and highlights the main principle taught or the theme developed in the article.

The articles themselves, as implied above, discuss their subjects with certain principles or lessons in mind. Each seeks to describe its subject and explain why the subject is important to American church history. Over half of the articles originally appeared in *FAITH for the Family* magazine, although several were written especially for this anthology. A list of the contributors to this collection is found at the end of the book.

At the close of this introduction, each section introduction, and each article are ''Suggestions for Further Reading.'' The works in these lists have been selected with the general reader in mind and are usually nontechnical and popular in style. Inclusion in the suggested reading lists, however, does not constitute unqualified endorsement of the contents of such works or of other works done by the authors or publishers. Annotations are sometimes attached to the suggestions to help guide the reader in his selections.

The editor hopes that this anthology will provide an interesting and inspirational introduction to American church history. If spiritual gifts are to be used for edifying the body of Christ, then writing should also serve to edify. Church history should not simply entertain; it should glorify God. English church historian Joseph Milner wrote, "To see and trace the goodness of God taking care of his Church in every age by his providence and grace, will be, to the devout mind, a refreshment of the most grateful nature." It is hoped that this work will be such a refreshment.

Suggestions for Further Reading

General Works

Sydney E. Ahlstrom. *A Religious History of the American People.* New Haven: Yale University Press, 1972.

Earle Cairns. *Endless Line of Splendor.* Wheaton: Tyndale House, 1986. [On the history of revivals]

Christian History is a quarterly magazine devoted to church history and similar to *American Heritage* in format and reading interest.

Edwin S. Gaustad. *A Documentary History of Religion in America.* 2 vols. Grand Rapids: Eerdmans, 1982, 1983.

Winthrop S. Hudson. *Religion in America.* 4th ed. New York: Macmillan, 1987.

George M. Marsden. *Religion and American Culture.* San Diego: Harcourt Brace Jovanovich, 1990.

Frank S. Mead. *Handbook of Denominations in the United States.* 9th ed. Revised by Samuel S. Hill. Nashville: Abingdon, 1990.

Mark A. Noll, et al., eds. *Eerdmans' Handbook to Christianity in America.* Grand Rapids: Eerdmans, 1983. [Possibly the best survey of American church history for the layperson]

William Warren Sweet. *The Story of Religion in America.* 1950. Reprint. Grand Rapids: Baker, 1973.

John D. Woodbridge, Mark A. Noll, and Nathan O. Hatch. *The Gospel in America: Themes in the Story of America's Evangelicals.* Grand Rapids: Zondervan, 1979.

General Denominational Histories

Lefferts A. Loetscher. *A Brief History of the Presbyterians.* 4th ed. Philadelphia: Westminster, 1978.

H. Leon McBeth. *The Baptist Heritage: Four Centuries of Baptist Witness.* Nashville: Broadman, 1987.

John T. McNeill. *History and Character of Calvinism.* London: Oxford University Press, 1954.

J. L. Neve. *A Brief History of the Lutheran Church in America.* Burlington, Iowa: German Literary Board, 1916.

Faith of Our Fathers: Scenes from American Church History

Frederick A. Norwood. *The Story of American Methodism.* Nashville: Abingdon, 1974.

William Warren Sweet. *The Story of American Methodism.* Rev. ed. Nashville: Abingdon, 1954.

Abdel Ross Wentz. *A Basic History of Lutheranism in America.* Rev. ed. Philadelphia: Fortress Press, 1964.

The Colonial Era
(1607 to 1776)

The period between the founding of the Jamestown colony and the American Revolution divides into two broad movements: the founding and establishing of Christianity in America in the seventeenth century and the Great Awakening in the eighteenth century.

The story of the founding of Christianity in America is the record of pioneers, as the New World provided a haven for oppressed Christians in Europe. Starting with the Pilgrims of Plymouth, several groups came to America to find a place where they could worship God freely and in peace. The Baptists, Presbyterians, Quakers, and Lutherans—to name a few of the largest groups—found across the ocean a freedom that they could have only dreamed of back in Europe. In addition, the Anglican church (eventually to become known as the Protestant Episcopal church) naturally came to the shores of these English colonies.

Undeniably, the most important group to settle in America were the Puritans of New England. By their large numbers and their distinctive theology, the Puritans were the most important formative influence on colonial American religion. Yet they are a group that is much misunderstood. Twentieth-century cynic H. L. Mencken defined a Puritan as "a person in constant dread that someone somewhere might be happy." Likewise, Americans who cherish their heritage of religious freedom are puzzled by a group that fled England because of religious oppression and then refused to allow any other group freedom of conscience.

John Winthrop, the first governor of the Massachusetts Bay Colony, provides an answer to this puzzle. In an address aboard the ship that brought him to the New World, Winthrop said, "We shall be as a city upon a hill, the eyes of all people are upon us; so that if we shall deal falsely with our God in this work we have undertaken and so cause him to withdraw his present help from us, we shall be made a story and a by-word through the world." The name *Puritan* comes from their desire to "purify" the Church of England of alleged Roman Catholic elements and to establish their reformed faith in England. In America, however, the Puritans could do more than *reform* a church and a nation; they could start from scratch. In building their "holy commonwealth," the

1

Faith of Our Fathers: Scenes from American Church History

Puritans wanted to construct a society based upon the strictures of the Bible. (Many modern "blue laws" requiring businesses to close on Sundays are a remnant of this Puritan influence on America.) Devotion to God and His purpose, they thought, required the strictest obedience to His Word. The Puritans could no more conceive of "freedom of religion" in their society than the modern Christian could conceive of allowing every range of heretical doctrine to flourish in his church.

Many Americans, knowing only the caricatures of Puritans by men such as Mencken, do not realize that the Puritans brought a sense of religious devotion and holy mission to these shores and enriched the heritage of this nation. The writings of the early Puritans show an intense piety, a fervent love for God, and a burning desire to please Him. Like nearly all movements in Christian history, however, they eventually suffered decline. A chief cause of decline was the "Half-Way Covenant." The Puritans (or Congregationalists, as they came to be known in New England) required a profession of personal faith in Christ for membership in their churches. Children of members, however, became members at their baptism. Many of these baptized descendants of the founders could not honestly make this profession when they came of age. In order to keep these people in the church, pastors devised the Half-Way Covenant, in which unsaved but outwardly moral church members could present their children for baptism (and hence membership). The result, unfortunately, was a growing number of unregenerate church members in New England's congregations. Puritan decline reached its nadir in 1692 in an orgy of fanaticism. A series of "witch trials" centering in Salem, Massachusetts, resulted in the execution of twenty people and the tarnishing of the colony's reputation.

Colonial religious decline was halted, however, by the first sweeping revival in American history, the Great Awakening. This revival shook America from the 1720s to the 1760s, although the height of the awakening came in 1740-1742. It began as a series of local awakenings. The first took place in a group of Dutch Reformed congregations in New Jersey's Raritan Valley under the ministry of the Rev. Theodore Frelinghuysen. Like a growing number of ministers, Frelinghuysen was convinced that Christianity was becoming a nominal formalism in the colonies. He stressed the necessity of heartfelt conversion and a holy life as an evidence of that conversion. His work inspired others to preach with the same fervor and results, notably Presbyterian Gilbert Tennent in the mid-Atlantic colonies.

Undoubtedly the most famous of these local leaders was Jonathan Edwards of Northampton, Massachusetts, America's first great theologian. His sermon "Sinners in the Hands of an Angry God" is probably the best-known literary work emerging from the revival, but he is even more important for the learned works he wrote defending the revival and explaining its nature. Indeed, Edwards may have been the first man to formulate a theology of revivalism.

These localized awakenings were united and made a truly national revival through the ministry of English evangelist George Whitefield. A powerful preacher who had already shaken England with the gospel, Whitefield made seven preaching tours throughout the colonies. These evangelistic campaigns not only harvested thousands of souls for Christ and transformed communities, but they also brought the previously scattered revivals into close contact and warm fellowship.

The revival reached other regions through the faithful ministries of other great—if sometimes lesser known—men of God. Presbyterian Samuel Davies preached with great power and results in Virginia, for example, and Baptist Shubal Stearns carried the awakening to the Carolinas. By crossing sectional lines, the Great Awakening was the first truly *national* movement in American history and provided an important step in the transformation of the British colonies of North America into the *United* States of America.

Suggestions for Further Reading

Edwin S. Gaustad. *The Great Awakening in New England.* New York: Harper, 1957.

Peter Marshall and David Manuel. *The Light and the Glory.* Old Tappan, N.J.: Revell, 1977.

Perry Miller. *Errand into the Wilderness.* Cambridge, Mass.: The Belknap Press of Harvard University Press, 1956.

Perry Miller and Thomas Johnson. *The Puritans.* 2 vols. 1938. Reprint. New York: Harper Torchbooks, 1963. [An anthology of Puritan writings with excellent introductory essays by Miller and Johnson]

Edmund S. Morgan. *The Puritan Dilemma: The Story of John Winthrop.* Boston: Little, Brown and Company, 1958. [Not only a fine biography of Winthrop but also an excellent history of the early days of the Massachusetts Bay Colony]

Mark Noll. *Christians in the American Revolution.* Grand Rapids: Christian University Press, 1977.

William Warren Sweet. *Religion in Colonial America.* New York: Charles Scribner's Sons, 1942.

Joseph Tracy. *The Great Awakening.* 1842. Reprint. Edinburgh: Banner of Truth Trust, 1976.

God's Man at Jamestown

by Gene Elliott

When Americans think of the religious beginnings of their nation, they naturally think first of the Pilgrims, the Plymouth colony, and the first Thanksgiving. Chronologically, however, the Jamestown settlement in 1607 predated that in Plymouth. Virginia did not have the ostensibly religious purpose in its founding that characterized the Pilgrim and later Puritan colonies in New England; profit admittedly played a larger role in the founding of Virginia. It would be a mistake, though, to think of Virginia as somehow "secular," untouched by the effects of Christianity. No man better exemplifies the deep religious devotion and purpose of many early settlers of Virginia than the first chaplain of the Jamestown colony, Robert Hunt.

It was 1607, Jamestown, Virginia. The Jamestown colony was in trouble. Most of the men were sick with malaria, and many of those who were well were spending their time as "proper" English gentlemen should—looking for pearls in oyster shells instead of working to meet the needs of the struggling colony. But there was one man, a preacher named Robert Hunt, who was conspicuously different. Every Sunday, from behind a plank nailed between two trees, he preached to a small congregation shaded under the canopy of an old sailcloth. During the week he cared for the sick and dying, and he labored more than his share of the time at the building tasks. How he had time to supervise the building of a grist mill, one only wonders. Were it not for this faithful servant, God might have written "Ichabod" over the entire colony.

Two facts stand out to the Christian who examines accounts of this early colony. First, God often received little mention or credit for working in the lives of men during that time, and second, the settlers had many more failures than successes.

Groundwork for the failure was laid early. In the late sixteenth century, many English preachers extolled a possible "noble evangelical outreach'' for colonizing the New World. But the quality of spiritual activity in England at the time did not encourage an outreach of this type. A primary interest on the part of most participants in the journey to the new land was to confiscate some of the gold and jewels supposedly possessed by the Indians. To many it was a ''get-rich-quick'' scheme.

A preview of coming disasters occurred in the late 1580s, when several attempts failed to establish a colony in what is now Virginia. Several groups remained to settle Roanoke Island, one later returning to England with Sir Francis Drake when their supplies ran low, and another remaining to settle there but vanishing without a trace.

It took several years before enough interest and funds were raised to warrant another expedition. In 1606, under a charter granted by King James, a group including Captain John Smith sailed from London. There was something strange about the passenger list: there were no women aboard! One doubts the stated purpose of the settlement as being ''evangelistic,'' for without wives and mothers, a permanent colony seemed out of the question. Likewise, it was strange that for an ''evangelistic'' effort, Hunt was the only minister aboard.

The one-hundred-ton *Susan Constant,* the forty-ton *Godspeed*, and the twenty-ton *Discovery* made their way in December 1606 to the east coast of England, where unfavorable weather held them near land for six weeks, only twenty miles from Hunt's home, causing valuable supplies to be consumed. Looking back to the beginning of the voyage, we see the effect that one life can have on 143 others. From the outset, Hunt's presence and spirituality directly affected the passengers in a positive way. Only a few days out from shore, he became ill. John Smith wrote that during this initial illness, few expected Hunt to live. Not only did he improve and live, however, but he also uttered no word of complaint, and his godly example quenched ''the flames of envy and discension'' among his shipmates.

Let us imagine the relationship of Hunt to his shipmates. It was clear that while he preached repentance from sin to his listeners, he exuded the qualities of a peacemaker. English gentlemen listened with irritation and impatience to this ''upstart'' preacher who told them they needed Jesus Christ, when they had not needed anything before in their lives except others to wait upon them. Indeed, they did not plan to lift a hand to unload the ship, and here was this clergyman telling them to become laborers in some kind of spiritual vineyard.

Once the ships reached the landing site on the James River, a seven-man council made the first of many unfortunate decisions: they did not build the colony above swamp level. The men contracted many serious diseases, including swamp fever (malaria). Despite the widespread physical ills, the lack of proper food, and the arrogance of ''gentlemen'' who would rather open oyster shells than work, Robert Hunt remained faithful to God and went about his work of preaching, doctoring, and building. If any man doubted the reality of Hunt's faith, he surely was no longer skeptical when, after the fire of 1608 that reduced to ashes all but three huts and half the supplies, Hunt offered no complaints, even though he lost everything but the shirt on his back.

Sometime between the fire and 1609, Hunt went to be with the Lord. The men lamented the passing of the "good Mr. Hunt." John Smith later penned these fitting words as a memorial:

> He was an honest, religious, and courageous Divine; he preferred the service of God to every thought of ease at home. He endured every privation, yet none ever heard him repine. During his life, our fractions were oft healed and our greatest extremities so comforted that they seemed easy in comparison with what we endured after his death. We all received from him the Holy Communion together as a pledge of reconciliation, for we loved him for his exceeding goodness. He planted the first Protestant church in America, and laid down his life in the foundation of Virginia.

From that time on disasters seemed more numerous. Only a partial crop was planted in 1609; rats and rot ruined the storehouse grain; and the starving people dispersed, seeking any food to survive. Only the arrival of Lord De La Warr in 1610 with additional settlers and supplies saved the remnant from total destruction.

Nearly four hundred years later, when Christians in the United States experience little privation or discomfort, it is good for us to remember this man of God and to take note of how he reacted to adverse conditions. Although God's blessing seemed missing at Jamestown, Robert Hunt labored faithfully. And although little is recorded about his life, mere paragraphs speak volumes to our hearts.

Suggestions for Further Reading

Perry Miller. "Religion and Society in the Early Literature of Virginia." In *Errand into the Wilderness*. Cambridge, Mass.: The Belknap Press of Harvard University Press, 1956, pp. 99-140. [An essay by a renowned historian of colonial religion discussing the importance of religion in the early Virginia colony]

The Pilgrims and God's Providence

by David O. Beale

Is any story in America's religious heritage better known than that of the Pilgrims and the first Thanksgiving? The following account of the Pilgrims and the circumstances behind that celebration demonstrates how much they had to thank God for. It also stresses that God's beneficent providence had brought them through far more than a single harsh winter to a plentiful harvest; Thanksgiving is the celebration of God's preserving grace for His people.

It was time to declare "a day of solemn humiliation" to seek God's guidance. The group of Separatist Christians had come to Leyden, Holland, from Scrooby, England, twelve years earlier. Now they were preparing to move to the New World, where they might carry the gospel, preserve their own language and culture, and bring up their children according to the dictates of their own consciences.

At Leyden, they gathered early at Pastor John Robinson's home in Bell Alley and heard him preach from Ezra 8:21: "Then I proclaimed a fast there, at the river of Ahava, that we might afflict ourselves before our God, to seek of him a right way for us, and for our little ones, and for all our substance." Robinson then declared it a day of fasting and prayer to prepare them for the arduous voyage ahead. At the day's end they enjoyed a farewell dinner of goose and pudding. One of the Pilgrims, Edward Winslow, described the scene: "We refreshed ourselves, after our tears, with the singing of Psalms, making joyful melody in our hearts as well as with the voice, there being many in the congregation very expert in music; and indeed it was the sweetest melody that ever mine ears have heard."

The next morning they boarded canal boats for the twenty-four mile trip to Delftshaven, Rotterdam, where the sixty-ton *Speedwell* would be waiting. As Leyden's red-tiled roofs, and spires, and great windmill receded into the distance, Pilgrim hearts flooded with tender memories— and perhaps some regrets. Some, like the Bradfords and the Winslows, had begun their married lives in Leyden. Any homesickness, however, was only momentary, as William Bradford himself explained: "And so they left that good and pleasant city, which had been their resting place near twelve years; but they knew they were pilgrims, and looked not much on these things, but lifted up their eyes to the heavens, their dearest country, and quieted their spirits."

At Delftshaven the voyagers spent the remainder of the day loading food and cargo into the *Speedwell*. William Brewster brought along his printing press and a library of almost two hundred books, including his beloved Geneva Bible, which would become a schoolbook for the young people.

Dawn on July 22, 1620, arrived with a fair wind, and it was time for final embraces. The Pilgrims knelt on the dock as Pastor Robinson solemnly invoked God's blessing on the mission. In a few minutes they were sailing for Southampton, England, where they would join the ninety-ton *Mayflower*.

The two ships sailed for the New World on August 5, 1620, but they were hardly three days at sea when the *Speedwell* began taking water. The voyagers turned back to Dartmouth for the ship's recaulking. After about a week they set sail again. Almost three hundred miles later, however, water was again rising in the *Speedwell's* hold. Once more they must turn back; this time they limped into Plymouth, where the *Speedwell* was finally declared unseaworthy. Her passengers and cargo would have to go aboard the *Mayflower*.

About twenty of the *Speedwell's* passengers willingly dropped out. God was using the ship's problems—whatever their human explanations—to separate chaff from wheat, or, as William Stoughton later put it, "God sifted a whole nation, that He might send choice grain into this wilderness." "Like Gideon's army," Bradford explained, "this small number was divided, as if the Lord, by this work of His providence, thought these few were still too many for the great work He had to do."

The *Mayflower,* with her six white sails in the wind, finally departed with 102 passengers. By now, however, it was September 6—more than a month behind schedule. The voyagers had already consumed the provisions calculated for the voyage, which would last at least two more months in an ill-lighted, rolling, stinking vessel. They were now eating food which they might need in order to stay alive in a wilderness in the dead of winter. They could not turn back. Having sold their houses and possessions, they had no place else to go.

Unmerciful harassment came from some of the sailors, whose self-appointed leader gloated at the Christians' seasickness and boasted that he would soon sew them all in shrouds and feed them to the fish. Ironically, this very crewman came down suddenly with a strange fever and died within a few hours. No one else contracted this "mysterious" disease, and his was the first shrouded body to go overboard. The mocking ceased.

One passenger nearly paid with his life for disobeying the order to remain below deck during the storms. During one prolonged storm, John Carver's servant, John Howland, could no longer endure the stench of the crowded living quarters. Climbing out onto the sea-swept main deck, Howland lost his balance and fell into the huge, boiling waves of the Atlantic. Providentially, the vessel was rolling over so far that the lines from her spars were trailing in the water. As one of these snaked across Howland's wrist, he instinctively grabbed it and hung on. Rescued from the jaws of death, Howland never again raised his head above the deck without an invitation.

The most terrifying moments came when the *Mayflower* was about halfway across the Atlantic. A violent storm was heeling the ship over dangerously. Children's screams were echoing through the lantern-lit darkness of the low-ceilinged 'tween-decks. Suddenly a tremendous sound of cracking timber resounded throughout the ship. The huge cross beam supporting the main mast had broken. The situation was desperate. Then someone remembered the great iron screw of Elder Brewster's printing press. They hauled the press into place beneath the beam and raised it back to its proper position. The printing press supported the beam the rest of the voyage. Praise ascended to God.

By now the food in the hold was almost inedible. Records indicate that the bread had to be broken with chisels. The cheese was hard and stale, the butter rancid. The peas and grain were inhabited with crawling things. The salt meat and fish had to be choked down. There was no fresh water, and the ale was rapidly becoming sour.

Near the end of the tenth week, William Butten, Dr. Samuel Fuller's twenty-two-year-old servant, took to his bunk with fever, agonizing pain, and stabbing lances of fire in his limbs. Before morning Butten was dead: it was the first case of scurvy. The young man had refused his master's warning to take the daily portion of lemon juice.

Finally, on November 9 at 7:00 in the morning, the Pilgrims heard a cry from the crow's-nest—"Land-Ho!" Tears of relief mingled with shouts of joy. Many fell on their knees in simple thanks to God. Then Elder Brewster suggested a song of praise, and the words of Psalm 100 soared from the crowded main deck. They were sixty-five days from Plymouth, ninety-seven from Southampton.

Captain Christopher Jones informed them that the long, low shore was part of a great arm of land called Cape Cod—far north of the territory which their patent entitled them to settle. With winter setting in along dangerous shoals, however, the expedition could spend no more time searching for the territory of the Virginia Company. Pastor Robinson had told them in his farewell letter to form a "body politic." Their own Scrooby Church Covenant would serve as a model for the Mayflower Compact.

As they had begun their long voyage by kneeling on the dock at Delftshaven to ask God's guidance, so they ended it by kneeling on the sands of Cape Cod to thank Him for His providence. Bradford marveled at

> this poor people's condition . . . no friends to welcome them, nor inns to entertain or refresh their weatherbeaten bodies, no houses . . . to repair to. . . . Whichever way they turned their eyes (save upward to the heavens) they could have little solace. . . . For summer being done, all things stand upon them . . . and the whole country, full of woods and thickets, represented a wild and savage hue. If they looked behind them, there was the mighty ocean. . . . What could now sustain them but the Spirit of God and His grace?

Providentially, they found land already cleared at "Plymouth." It seemed as if some unseen friend had prepared this very spot in anticipation of their arrival, but more storm clouds of trials were yet to come.

The first winter was dreadfully bitter. By April 1621 the Pilgrims had lost twenty-eight of their forty-eight male adults, including Governor John Carver. When the worst was finally over, forty-seven people had died, nearly half of their original number. They buried their dead at night in shallow unmarked graves so that the Indians could not know their losses. But God's hand of mercy guided the struggling colony to survival and fulfillment. Governor Bradford said, "They fetched them wood, made them fires, dressed them meat, made their beds, washed their loathsome clothes. . . . In a word, did all the homely and necessary offices . . . which dainty and queasy stomachs cannot endure . . . and all this willingly and cheerfully, without any grudging in the least, showing herein their true love unto their friends and brethren; a rare example and worthy to be remembered."

The high point of their week was Sunday worship, held in the blockhouse at the top of the hill. Four cannons from the *Mayflower* stood in place on the flat roof. Inside, on roughhewn log benches, the men sat on the left, the women on the right, as Elder Brewster preached "powerfully and profitable."

One day an Indian walked into camp speaking English. "Welcome!" he said in a deep resonant voice. His name was Samoset, an Algonquin who had learned English from various fishing captains. The story he told gave the Pilgrims cause to thank God once again for His providence.

According to Samoset, this area had been the territory of the Patuxets, a large hostile tribe who had killed every white man who landed on these shores. Just four years prior to the Pilgrim's landing a mysterious plague had devastated the entire tribe. Convinced that some great spirit had destroyed the Patuxets, neighboring tribes had shunned the entire area. So the cleared land on which the Pilgrims had settled actually belonged to no one. Their nearest neighbors, explained Samoset, were the Wampanoags some fifty miles to the southwest. These Indians numbered about sixty warriors, and Massasoit, their chief, also ruled over several other tribes.

Samoset returned to Plymouth the following week with another English-speaking Indian named Squanto. Squanto and Samoset soon arranged a meeting between Massasoit and the Pilgrims. From this meeting came a peace treaty which would last for forty years.

In October of 1621 Governor Bradford declared a day of public thanksgiving. From their gardens, the Pilgrims could now enjoy turnips, cabbages, carrots, onions, parsnips, cucumbers, radishes, and beets. They invited Massasoit, who arrived not only with ninety hungry Indians, but also with several dressed deer and wild turkeys. They taught the Pilgrim women how to make hoecakes and pudding from cornmeal and how to make maple syrup. The Pilgrims used the Indians' dried fruits to introduce them to blueberry and apple pies. All enjoyed the games that followed. It was a joyous occasion indeed.

The most memorable moment, however, was Elder Brewster's humble prayer to God, whose providence had guided and protected them in mercy. "We have noted these things," said Bradford, "so that you might see their worth and not negligently lose what your fathers have obtained with so much hardship."

Suggestions for Further Reading

William Bradford. *Of Plymouth Plantation*. Edited by Samuel Eliot Morison. New York: Alfred A. Knopf, 1952. [Numerous other editions of Bradford's work are also available.]

Thomas J. Fleming. *One Small Candle: The Pilgrims' First Year in America*. New York: W. W. Norton & Company, 1964.

Crispin Gill. *Mayflower Remembered: A History of the Plymouth Pilgrims*. New York: Taplinger Publishing Co., 1970.

George F. Willison. *Saints and Strangers*. New York: Reynal & Hitchcock, 1945.

Anne Bradstreet: Puritan Poet

by Karen Guffey

*Overshadowing the Pilgrims of Plymouth in ultimate impor-
tance in American history were the Puritans who settled most of
New England. Determined to build on America's shores "a city
upon a hill," a model society under the rule of God, the Puritans
began coming in large numbers in the 1630s to establish their
"holy commonwealth" on Massachusetts Bay. These hardy saints,
who (to borrow a remark from Bismarck) "feared God and nothing else," included many courageous believers, notably John Winthrop, the first governor. Among their number was a young woman
whose fame would grow in the centuries after her death because of
her faithful use of God's gifts. That woman was Anne Bradstreet.*

She is called the grandmother of American literature, and her literary
works mark the beginning of poetry and prose written by women in the
American colonies. Today a smattering of her works can be found in
most American literature anthologies. Anne Bradstreet is indeed a familiar name to students of literature, but she is much more. What is
often less remembered is the fact that she left the testimony of being a
godly woman whose greatest desire was to serve God not only by her
writing but also by loving and honoring her husband and rearing children
who would fear the Lord.

Anne was born in 1612 to Thomas and Dorothy Dudley of Northamp-
tonshire, England. Anne's father, a devout Puritan and a relatively well-
educated man for his day, encouraged his daughter's quest for knowledge.
When her father served as steward to the earl of Lincolnshire, Anne took
advantage of her access to the earl's library. She loved to read, and apparently one of her favorite works was Sir Walter Raleigh's *History of the
World*. More important, at the age or six or seven, she became an avid
reader of the Bible, which in turn created in Anne what she described as a
desire to "avoid sin, and turn toward righteousness."

During her early adolescence, Anne gave in to what she called the
"vanity and follies of youth," a frivolous lifestyle with little thought of
anything spiritual. A bout with smallpox at the age of sixteen drew her

back into close communion with God, but with this reconsecration began a series of battles with the Devil. "Many times hath Satan troubled me concerning the verity of the Scriptures," she noted as one example, and she mentioned how he also tempted her with thoughts of "Atheisme," that is "how I could know whether there was a God." Like many of the Puritans, Anne's life followed this pattern: very human doubts plagued her but her faith in God always triumphed and emerged stronger.

In 1621 Simon Bradstreet, a young graduate of Cambridge (a center of Puritan teaching), was employed as an assistant to Anne's father in the earl's estate. Three years after Bradstreet's arrival, Anne's family moved to Boston, England, but the two young people apparently kept in contact. Their friendship blossomed into love, and in 1628—in Anne's own words—"I changed my condition and was married."

Her condition was to change in more than her marital status. The Puritans were suffering increased persecution from government authorities for their desire to reform the Church of England. Many Puritans, including Simon Bradstreet, decided to found a colony in British North America where they could worship God as they pleased. After only two years of marriage, the Bradstreets sailed for Massachusetts. In England Anne had been acquainted with many dignitaries and learned people; she had enjoyed a life of relative ease. The Massachusetts Bay colony, however, was struggling for survival when she and her husband arrived in 1630. Many people were ill, and supplies were low. Only when she became "convinced it was the way of God" was Anne able to adjust to the rugged life of the New World.

Five or six years of marriage passed before the first child, Samuel, was born into the Bradford home, and other children followed until Anne found herself a busy mother of eight. ("I had eight birds hatcht in one nest," she wrote in one of her poems.) She also somehow found time to write. Anne never intended her works to be published, but her brother-in-law gathered several of her poems and had them published in England under the title *The Tenth Muse*. The volume was not well received, and Anne later referred to the book as her "rambling brat" and as "Thou ill-form'd offspring of my feeble brain."

Most of Anne Bradstreet's poems were undiscovered until years after her death. Because she wrote for her own pleasure and for her family's instruction, her works lack the artificial tone that probably would have been characteristic of poetry intended for the public eye. Her poems are simple, straightforward expressions of her emotions—her love for her husband, her children, and her God; her grief at her losses and trials. For example, she wrote in "To My Dear and Loving Husband":

If ever two were one, then surely we.
If ever man were lov'd by wife, then thee:

If ever wife was happy in a man,
Compare with me ye women if ye can.
I prize thy love more than whole Mines of gold,
Or all the riches that the earth doth hold.
My love is such that Rivers cannot quench,
Nor ought but love from thee, give recompence.
Thy love is such I can no way repay.
The heavens reward thee manifold I pray.
Then while we live, in love let's so persever,
That when we live no more, we may live ever.

Her faith also shone through her works. Anne's poetry is a reflection not only of herself but also of the era in which she lived. The Puritans believed that God was revealed through His creation, a belief reflected in her poem ''Contemplations'':

I wist not what to wish, yet sure thought I,
If so much excellence abide below,
How excellent is He that dwells on high,
Whose power and beauty by His works we know?

In 1656, thinking she was near death, Anne began keeping a journal. Not wanting to die without passing on to her children the wisdom she had gained from her spiritual battles, she wrote of her experiences with God, especially of her chastisements. She wrote that God had dealt graciously with her, revealing the victory she had won over her doubts.

Anne suffered many losses in the New World. On a night in July 1666, she awoke to find her house on fire. It was destroyed—along with most of the family possessions–and Anne poured out her thoughts on paper. Grieved but not bitter, she wrote:

To my God my heart did cry
To strengthen me in my distress. . . .
And when I could no longer look,
I blest His name that gave and took. . . .
It was His own, it was not mine.

Another tragedy followed in 1669. One of Anne's grandsons, only one month old, died, ''cropt by th' Almighties hand.'' Filled with sorrow, she nevertheless wrote in relation to his death, ''Let's say [God is] merciful as well as just. He will return, and make up our losses.'' Such simple but profound expression of faith in God carried Anne through all difficulties. Whatever sorrows and disappointments she faced, her writing remained positive in tone. Rather than complain, she praised the omniscient God who brought her through the darker periods of life.

Faith of Our Fathers: Scenes from American Church History

Anne Bradstreet died on September 16, 1672. Her poetry, published long after her death, brought her literary recognition, but fame was not her goal. Writing was to her simply an outlet for love, sorrow, and faith—a means of praising God. Her final poem, written three years before her death, reveals her unfailing trust in an unfailing God:

Oh how I long to be at rest
And soar on high among the blest.
Such lasting joy shall there behold
As ear ne'er heard, nor tongue 'ere told.
Lord make me ready for that day
Then come dear Bridgroom come away.

Suggestions for Further Reading

The Complete Works of Anne Bradstreet. Edited by Joseph R. McElrath, Jr., and Allan P. Robb. Boston: Twayne, 1981.

Samuel Eliot Morison. "Mistress Anne Bradstreet," Chapter 11 in *Builders of the Bay Colony.* Boston: Houghton Mifflin, 1930, pp. 320-26.

Raymond A. St. John. *American Literature for Christian Schools.* Greenville, S.C.: Bob Jones University Press. [Pages 60-70 discuss Anne Bradstreet's works and give selections from her writings.]

John Eliot: Apostle to the Indians

by Sandra Harber

Historians often label Englishman William Carey "the Father of Modern Missions" and consider Adoniram Judson the great pioneer of American missions in particular. Predating both, however, was Puritan John Eliot whose work among the Algonquin Indians of New England was both a story of the triumph of God's grace and one of the few bright chapters in the unhappy story of Indian-white relations in North America.

Twentieth-century Christians usually look with awe upon missionaries who leave comfortable America to serve the Lord in remote jungles among primitive tribes. "What fine Christian courage!" they remark. But one of North America's first missionaries was called foolhardy when he went to minister to people only a few miles from his home.

John Eliot was a pastor in Roxbury, Massachusetts, who ventured from his secure Bay Colony settlement into the surrounding hostile forest in the mid-seventeenth century to evangelize the Indians. Many of his fellow Puritan settlers regarded their Indian neighbors with terror; they feared death-dealing raids on frontier families and looked with horror on the pagan powwows. The bravery of the "Apostle to the Indians," however, sprang from his sure faith in his heavenly Father's protection. Once, while on a solitary ride to an Indian village, the daring preacher was confronted by a knife-wielding warrior. His dark eyes meeting those of the Indian, Eliot stated simply, "I am about the work of the great God, and he is with me, so that I fear not all the sachems [chiefs] of the country. I'll go on, and do you touch me if you dare." John Eliot continued on his journey unmolested.

Cambridge-trained

The character of a man who could calmly defy an Indian's threat to his life was forged in a time of great religious turmoil. John Eliot was born the third of seven children on July 31, 1604, in Essex County, England. Bennett Eliot, a fairly well-to-do landholder, taught his children a deep reverence for God and His Word. His missionary son later testified to the Eliot's Christian home life: "I do see that it was a great favour of God unto me, to season my first times with the fear of God, the word, and prayer."

From 1618 to 1622 Eliot studied for the ministry at Cambridge University, the intellectual center of Puritanism. When the talented young theologian graduated, he accepted a teaching position in a small school in the obscure village of Little Baddow. Here Eliot lived and taught under Thomas Hooker, a Puritan clergyman (and later the founder of Connecticut) who firmly believed that people should be allowed to worship as they pleased. The brief period Eliot spent with the Hooker family seemed to mark a turning point in his relationship to Jesus Christ. Eliot wrote of his stay with Thomas and his wife Susanna: "Here the Lord said to my dead soul, live! live! and through the grace of God I do live and shall live forever! When I came to this blessed family I then saw as never before, the power of godliness in its lovely vigor and efficacy."

The situation for those who did not conform to the standards laid down by the bishops of the Anglican church grew worse. Hooker was finally forced to flee to Holland in 1630, from where he later sailed to Massachusetts. The sudden departure of his good friend left Eliot at a crossroads. He saw a future of teaching and preaching in the New World, while the Old seemed to offer only exile from the ministry or a jail cell. So in the later summer of 1631 Eliot boarded the ship *Lyon,* bound for Boston.

Pastor in a New World

John Eliot began his ministry in America as substitute pastor of the church in Boston. His parishioners were pleased with his preaching, but when part of Eliot's family and friends settled two miles away in Roxbury, he moved to their village and became pastor of the First Church of Roxbury. In 1632 his fiancée, Hanna Mumford, whom he was said to have met in Little Baddow, sailed to America. Their marriage in October of that year was, according to Roxbury records, the first in the new settlement.

John Eliot became a powerful minister and a compassionate pastor to the New Englanders in Roxbury. His sermons, according to Boston minister Cotton Mather, displayed "a most penetrating liveliness" and resembled "God's trumpets of wrath against all vice." Eliot's generous nature became so notorious that he was once handed a month's salary securely knotted in a handkerchief, with the hope that he would be able to hold on to it a little longer. On his way home, however, Eliot stopped at the home of a poor widow, for whom he vainly attempted to extract a coin from his bundle. Abandoning the struggle, he gave her the handkerchief, declaring, "I think the Lord meant it all for you." This incident was typical of Eliot's fifty-eight years in the Roxbury pastorate—years when he and his people peacefully served the Lord together.

Learning Algonquin

When the New Englanders were granted their charters for land in the New World, they promised to take the gospel to the Indians. But most of the first colonists did not fulfill their glowing pledges to evangelize the natives. The Indians appeared to find talk of God "burdensome," and their lives seemed dominated by satanic rituals. For their part, the new settlers found their lives too filled with plowing the land, building homes, and caring for the sick to take the time to preach to their neighbors in the forest villages.

But John Eliot's compassion extended to the Indians. During his first year at Roxbury he saw them as lost, needy souls. At this time he wrote: "We are at good peace with the . . . natives . . . and I trust, in God's time they shall larne Christ." Eliot's single-minded sense of mission to the Indians helped him overcome the barrier of the Algonquin language. He had shown a flair for languages at Cambridge, where he had been especially interested in Greek, Hebrew, and linguistics. In talking with Indians in Roxbury and the surrounding countryside, Eliot had picked up numerous "everyday words" of the Algonquin language. But Eliot's goal was not mere conversation; he wanted to explain God's Word to the natives. The language the preacher wanted to learn was totally different from any European or classical tongue. Algonquin had no written grammar, no written dictionary. Cockenoe, Eliot's young Indian teacher, could speak English fluently but could not write. Only Eliot's dedication kept him going for the two grueling years that he studied Algonquin.

On October 28, 1646, at Nonantum, Eliot preached his first sermon to the Indians, using Ezekiel 37:9 as his text. He opened the service with a prayer in English, not wanting to use "some unfit or unworthy terms in the solemn office." Then, for the first time in an Indian tongue, he explained the Ten Commandments, the creation and fall of man, and the life and character of Christ. At the close of his sermon, Eliot asked his intent listeners for questions. Almost immediately he was asked, "How may we come to know Jesus Christ?" Eliot's answer was clear: repent, pray, and receive Christ as Saviour.

In this meeting, as in later ones, Eliot assured his concerned listeners that God heard prayers in Algonquin just as He heard those offered in English. He encouraged his converts to trust God instead of consorting with the tribal sorcerers who enjoyed a reign of terror over the natives. Because of his emphasis on prayer, Eliot's converts became known as "praying Indians."

The Praying Villages

The Indians invited Eliot to return and preach to them again, and they also requested land on which to build a town. It was this request which brought Eliot both his greatest success and his greatest hardship in his missionary work. Eliot had already encountered opposition from some Indian chiefs who feared they were losing the loyalty of the converted warriors. But some New Englanders also doubted the value of Eliot's work. Most of the English who settled the New World believed that all land uncultivated by the Indians belonged to the king and could therefore be parceled out only by the crown or its representatives. The Indians, accustomed to ranging over the land at will, found the colonists' attitude hard to understand. John Eliot, however, was determined not to let the dispute over land claims deter him from his desire to separate his converts from hostile Indians and suspicious settlers. He felt it was necessary for the Algonquins to live in a town so that they could be "under the government of the Lord, and . . . have a church." He was also concerned that the Indians be in a community where they could more easily be instructed in such skills as reading, writing, planting, and building. His arguments proved convincing to the Massachusetts General Court, and that body granted the Indians six thousand acres for their first town.

After a fruitless search for the perfect location, Eliot got on his knees before God. It was while he was still praying that one of his Indian converts came to his teacher and led him to the future site of the first "praying village": Natick. The Indians built the town, including wigwams, a storehouse, a meetinghouse, a fort, and a footbridge without any other aid than that of an English carpenter, who was there for two days. They based their civil government on the Mosaic plan in Exodus 18: rulers of tens, fifties, and hundreds. Eliot composed the town's formal laws himself, and the Indians soon became conscientious in rebuking and punishing those who broke laws such as abstaining from strong drink.

Eliot traveled to Natick at least once every two weeks. His converts multiplied, and by 1656 all of the house lots at Natick had been assigned, leaving no room for other Christian Indians. As a result, thirteen more towns were established in Massachusetts' Nipmuck County. The hardworking missionary needed assistance in overseeing the government of the villages; so the Massachusetts General Court, which Eliot had kept informed of the progress, appointed Daniel Gookin as superintendent of all the praying villages. Gookin had participated in planting the Virginia and Maryland colonies. When religious persecution arose in those settlements, he moved to Massachusetts where he became a steadfast friend to Eliot.

The Indian Library

Eliot not only continued to preach to the Indians but also worked in other ways for their benefit. As a scholar, he placed great emphasis on education, and as a missionary, he realized that others were needed to carry on his work. In 1671 Eliot wrote: "I find few English students willing to engage in so dim a Work as this." Thus, Eliot established schools for the Christian Indians and trained them to be teachers and pastors of their own people. These schools were successful, as Cotton Mather testified in *Magnalia Christi Americana* when he quoted his father, Increase Mather: "Of the Indian there are four-and-twenty who are preachers of the Word of God."

For use in his schools the able linguist published an Indian primary and catechism as well as many other works. These became part of what Cotton Mather labeled the "Indian library." Eliot's greatest contribution to this library was his translation of the entire Bible into Algonquin.

It was a difficult task, and Eliot encountered many problems in his attempt to provide an accurate, literal translation. The Indian culture was far removed from the Jewish culture of the Bible. Indian males were expected to be chaste; therefore, the ten virgins in Matthew 25 became ten chaste young men awaiting the Bridegroom. Another problem was finding Indian words that corresponded to the English. The Indian vocabulary lacked the abstract words required to explain spiritual concepts, and Eliot struggled to find the Indian comparisons to the often figurative English version. Sometimes he even had difficulty finding matching concrete nouns. One example was the word "lattice" a framework made of crossed pieces of wood. The closest word in Algonquin to fit this definition was "eelpot," a cage made of twigs and bark which was used to catch fish. But, in applying this to Judges 5:28, the result was: "The mother of Sisera looked out at a window, and cried through the eelpot." Eliot wisely chose to let the English "lattice" stand.

After eight grueling years the Indian translation was complete. In 1663 the first Bible printed in America came off the presses. J. H. Trumbull, a nineteenth-century expert in North American Indian dialects, said of the Algonquin Bible: "On the whole, his [Eliot's] version was probably as good as any first version that has been made, from his time to ours, in a previously unwritten and so-called 'barbarous' language." Eliot himself didn't seem to feel he could now rest from his arduous translation labors. In 1663 he wrote in a letter to a friend: "My work about the Indian Bible being finished, I am meditating what to do next for these Sons of our Morning [Indians]: they having no books for their private use." Eliot went on to translate some devotional and sermon books for the praying Indians.

King Philip's War

Every mission work suffers its share of setbacks, and John Eliot's pioneer effort was no exception. Although the majority of the Christian Indians were loyal to the English, the relationship between the other tribes and the settlers had for a long time been like a powder keg waiting for a match. But it was the murder of one of the praying Indians which lit the fuse and blew the keg. Sassamon, once a student in Eliot's Natick school, had become a secretary to King Philip, chieftain of the Wampanoag tribe. He then moved back to Natick, was converted, and became the village schoolmaster. Now loyal to the English, Sassamon went to Plymouth Governor Winslow to warn that Philip was planning a campaign against the colony. A few days later Sassamon's body was found in a pond near his home. The Wampanoag murderers were found, tried, and hanged. King Philip used the execution of his tribesmen as an excuse for attacking the Massachusetts town of Swansea on June 24, 1675. The war had begun.

Eliot and his assistant Gookin planned to use the praying Indian villages as a line of defense, and several hundred of the Christian natives joined the English army and taught the white man how to cope with Indian tactics. However, the settlers soon became panicky at even the sight of a red face, and the General Court exiled the praying Indians to Deer Island in Boston harbor. Eliot and Gookin visited them frequently to offer whatever aid and comfort they could. But many Indians died there from exposure and lack of food.

In 1677, 162 Christian Indians returned to the four surviving towns. The war had made the Indians contemptible in the colonists's eyes and had made the English lose what little desire they had once possessed to Christianize the Indians. One Englishman even reported that the war was caused by "an imprudent zeal . . . to Christianize those heathen before they were civilized." John Eliot, now seventy-two, became the target of abuse by many of his fellow New Englanders. But even as the older praying Indians died and new converts were few, Eliot continued to visit the towns every two weeks until he was physically unable to ride. Nor did he neglect his Roxbury parish, preaching to his faithful congregation until he could no longer walk to the church. Indian and Negro children still came to his home for lessons.

The Father of Modern Missions

John Eliot left this world for a better one on May 20, 1690. The remaining villages and the Natick church, already depleted by King Philip's War, now dwindled rapidly. After the church's Indian preacher Daniel Tokkowampait died in 1716, English clergymen led the decreasing assembly.

John Eliot: Apostle to the Indians

Was this dedicated missionary's work for naught, thwarted by a brief war started by an insignificant tribal chieftain? No—John Eliot not only led numerous Indians to accept Jesus Christ as Saviour, but his missionary endeavor also set a pattern which perhaps earns him the title "Father of Modern Missions." Says one writer: "The American Indian mission . . . provided both inspiration and a model for the nineteenth-century advance. . . . The young churches of Asia, Africa, and the Pacific islands are in a very real sense the fruits of the ministry of John Eliot." Not only have John Eliot's intense dedication and methods of establishing churches remained a pattern but also his means of financial support. In London the first Protestant missionary society, the Society for the Propagation of the Gospel in New England, was established for Eliot's financial benefit in 1649. It later grew into a worldwide mission.

Eliot left a bountiful legacy in other ways as well. The praying Indian villages survived him under English names such as Marlboro, Grafton, and Littleton. Natick kept its Indian name. The Roxbury Latin School, the grammar school Eliot founded, is still in operation. The Algonquin Bible and *Bay Psalm Book,* which Eliot co-authored with Richard Mather and Thomas Welch in 1640, are collector's items. Eliot's Indian grammar, which gives principles for tackling an unwritten language with no grammatical rules, has been studied and used in the formation of laws for the comparative science of linguistics.

John Eliot stands as a tremendous example of what one man can accomplish when his life is dedicated to Christ. But his underlying motive for everything he did was to glorify God, not himself. Said the "Apostle to the Indians" while on his deathbed: "My doings! Alas, they have been poor and small, and lean doings, and I'll be the man that shall throw the first stone at them all."

Suggestions for Further Reading

Samuel Eliot Morison. "John Eliot, Apostle to the Indians," Chapter 10 in *Builders of the Bay Colony.* Boston: Houghton Mifflin, 1930, pp. 289-319.

Francis Russell. "Apostle to the Indians." *American Heritage,* December 1957, pp. 4-9, 117-19.

Ola Winslow. *John Eliot, "Apostle to the Indians."* Boston: Houghton Mifflin Company, 1968.

Roger Williams:
Founder of Rhode Island

by David O. Beale and Mark Sidwell

Many American denominations look back to a "pioneer" re-
sponsible for establishing its group in this country. Presbyterians
honor Francis Makemie (subject of the next article), Lutherans
remember Henry Melchior Mühlenburg, and the German Reformed
recall Michael Schlatter. Of all the denominational founders, how-
ever, the one most likely to be found in secular history texts is Roger
Williams. His political as well as his religious importance makes
him an outstanding figure in American history.

He helped found Rhode Island; yet he often bore the brunt of hostility from the squabbling settlers of that tiny colony. He was a leading
figure in the establishment of the Baptists in America; yet he remained
with that denomination only a few months. He was an early advocate
of religious toleration; yet he wrote fiery polemics against theological
opponents. The founder of an American colony, an American denomination, and an American ideal, Roger Williams was a complex but
pivotal figure in the history of the United States.

Born in England around 1600, Roger Williams early came under the
generous patronage of the famed jurist Sir Edward Coke (1552-1634),
author of the 1628 Petition of Right (which reaffirmed the Magna Carta's
guarantees against imprisonment without due process of law) and advocate of the sovereignty of common law. Coke helped sponsor Williams's
education at Pembroke College, Cambridge. Receiving the B.A. degree
in 1627, Williams continued for two years of graduate training, after
which he received ordination as a minister. Abandoning a promising future in the Church of England, Williams became a Separatist, one who
believed that reform of the Anglican church was impossible and that true
Christians must form their own separate churches. Immediately he came
under the persecuting hand of Bishop William Laud of London. To avoid
arrest, he immigrated to New England in February 1631.

Roger Williams: Founder of Rhode Island

In Boston, Williams declined an invitation to become minister at First Church, because he found it "an unseparated church" (i.e., from the Church of England), and he said that he "durst not officiate to" it. After a brief visit to Salem, Williams went down to Plymouth, where he served in the Pilgrims' First Church. Williams also spent much time in Plymouth preaching to the Indians, learning their language, and even translating portions of Scripture into their tongue. "God was pleased," testified Williams, "to give me a painful, patient spirit, to lodge with them in their filthy, smoky holes . . . to gain their tongue." His "soul's desire" was "to do the natives good."

In the summer of 1633, Williams returned to Salem and served (unofficially) as Pastor Samuel Skelton's assistant. When Skelton died within a few weeks, Williams became acting pastor. Because Williams met with fierce opposition from the Massachusetts authorities, the Salem church did not formally install him as pastor until May 1635, and even then it was against the magistrates' wishes.

The opposition of the Massachusetts Bay magistrates resulted from Roger Williams's defense of five basic tenets. (1) The Church of England is apostate and any fellowship with it is disobedience to God. (2) The Massachusetts charter is wrong to refer to King Charles I as a "Christian." (To Williams, the king more closely resembled the apocalyptic Beast in the book of Revelation.) (3) The colony should abolish its required "Citizens' Oath" which forces unregenerate people to pledge loyalty to Christ and to attend Lord's Day services. (4) Civil magistrates should have no authority in spiritual matters pertaining to local churches (i.e., separation of church and state). (5) The Indians are the rightful owners of the land. Since these tenets undercut the very basis of Massachusetts's government and society, Williams appeared to be not simply a religious objector but a political revolutionary. Such "seditious doctrines" caused the magistrates in October 1635 to issue a decree of banishment—effective January 1636. With such an order, the authorities could arrest Williams and deport him back to England. Williams fled.

Accompanied by a few faithful friends, Williams traveled southward. "I was sorely tossed for . . . fourteen weeks, in a bitter winter season, not knowing what bread or bed did mean." Finally, on land which he purchased from the Indians along Narragansett Bay, Williams established the settlement he called "Providence," which became the core of the eventual colony of Rhode Island. Here at Providence Plantation, in 1639, Williams established the church that some consider to be the first Baptist church in America.

Williams, however, did not remain with the church which he founded. Four months after the church's establishment, Williams broke all denominational ties, believing that since Emperor Constantine's day (A.D.

306-337) all churches have remained in various degrees of apostasy. Williams did maintain a friendly relationship with the Baptists, but from that time he devoted his entire life to teaching the Indians.

He had a rare gift for languages. At Cambridge University, he had learned Latin, Greek, Hebrew, French, and Dutch. In Salem, Massachusetts, he had remarkably mastered the Narragansett Indian tongue. Finally, in 1643, Roger Williams published his *Key into the Language of America,* the first of his numerous works. Accurately described by one of Williams's biographers as "the first comprehensive book-length attempt in English to put the Indian language into print," *The Key* also includes abundant first-hand knowledge of the Indians' religion and customs.

Williams is rightly praised today for his advocacy of religious toleration. In his book *The Bloudy Tenent of Persecution for the Cause of Conscience,* an attack on the religious policies of Massachusetts, Williams wrote, "God requires not a uniformity of religion to be enacted and enforced in any civil state; which enforced uniformity, sooner or later, is the greatest occasion of civil war, ravishing of conscience, persecution of Christ Jesus in his servants, and of the hypocrisy and destruction of millions of souls. The permission of other consciences and worships than a state professeth only can, according to God, procure a firm and lasting peace." When Williams advocated the separation of church and state, however, he was not enunciating the modern idea of "protecting" the state from any religious influence. Instead he sought to shield the church from the power of government, an abuse he had experienced firsthand in both old and New England.

His belief in liberty of conscience did not make Williams hold his own beliefs any less dear or less important. In later years he continued a war of polemics with his religious opponents. When Puritan John Cotton of Massachusetts responded to *The Bloudy Tenent of Persecution* with a work of his own, *The Bloudy Tenent Washed and Made White in the Bloud of the Lambe,* the undaunted Williams answered with *The Bloudy Tenet Yet More Bloudy.* When Quaker George Fox toured the American colonies, the fiery Williams dashed off a polemic against Quaker teachings, the punningly titled *George Fox Digg'd Out of His Burrowes.* (Not to be outdone, Fox replied to Williams with *A New-England Fire-Brand Quenched.)*

Williams died in 1683. A little more than a century later, in 1791, the government of the United States adopted the following as the first sentence of the First Amendment of its Bill Rights: "Congress shall make no law respecting an establishment of religion, or prohibiting the free exercise thereof." It is not stretching the case to suggest that inspiration for that sentence lay at least in part in the life and labors of Roger Williams.

Suggestions for Further Reading

Edwin S. Gaustad. *Liberty of Conscience: Roger Williams in America.* Grand Rapids: Eerdmans, 1991.

Perry Miller. *Roger Williams: His Contribution to the American Tradition.* Indianapolis: Bobbs-Merrill, 1953. [Not so much a biography as selections from Williams's writings with appropriate commentary by Miller]

Ola Winslow. *Master Roger Williams, A Biography.* New York: The Macmillan Company, 1957.

Francis Makemie:
Champion of Religious Liberty

by David O. Beale and Terry Kane

The career of Francis Makemie in some ways parallels that of Roger Williams. Both men are credited with helping found major denominations in America (Williams the Baptists and Makemie the Presbyterians), and both were champions of religious liberty. That Makemie is less known today is perhaps because he, unlike Williams, extended himself more on behalf of his church than on behalf of religious liberty. Both causes were dearly important to Makemie, however, and America's religious history is richer for his contribution to both.

Over three hundred years ago in 1683, a dedicated twenty-five-year-old Scotch-Irish Presbyterian missionary landed at Colonel William Stevens's wharf on the west bank of the Pocomoke River on Maryland's Eastern Shore. The young man's name was Francis Makemie (mah-KIM-ee), and he came from the north of Ireland in answer to a letter that Colonel Stevens, a member of Lord Baltimore's Council, had sent three years earlier to the presbytery of Laggan, Ireland, requesting an evangelist for the Eastern Shore.

Francis Makemie, whose parents had been among the Covenanters who emigrated from Scotland to Northern Ireland during the reign of Charles II, was born near Ramelton in Donegal County, Ulster, about 1657. At the age of fourteen, under a godly schoolmaster's instruction, Makemie had "felt the influence of the Holy Spirit" in his soul. In 1681 the presbytery of Laggan licensed him to preach and sent him as a missionary first to Barbados, then on to America in response to Colonel Stevens's request. Makemie's reputation as a wise and godly missionary had preceded him to America. For months his coming was one of the chief topics of conversation among the plantations along the Maryland and Virginia shores.

Maryland, at this time under Lord Baltimore, enjoyed complete religious liberty. In Virginia, however, the government provided for the clergy of the established Church of England. The annual cost of such support was ten pounds of tobacco and a bushel of corn from every person sixteen years old and up. When Colonel Stevens asked Makemie how he planned to earn a living, the indomitable Ulsterman replied, "My first duty is to preach the gospel and to plant churches where there are none, but I have no fear as to how I shall live . . . . The truth is, I would much prefer to start at the bottom as any other immigrant."

Wherever Makemie preached, the crowds came—men, women, and children—eager to catch every word that the young minister spoke. Some came by boat, some on horseback, some in ox-carts; others trekked many miles on foot. Even the Indians came.

Although Makemie kept few written records during these years, numerous court records and family journals and traditions offer fleeting glimpses of "the man of God," as the Indians called him, riding or leading his horse "Button" along the seaside and bayside trails, going from one settlement to another. His sloop, *Tabitha,* became a familiar sight along the rivers and inlets throughout the Eastern Shore area. About 1690 Makemie married Naomi, the eldest daughter of William Anderson, a wealthy merchant of Accomack County, Virginia. Anderson bequeathed much of his wealth to Francis and Naomi.

This propitious beginning launched one of the most brilliant and dramatic careers in all of church history. As an itinerant evangelist, Makemie traveled at his own expense, but as an astute businessman he eventually enjoyed success in the West India trade. He was well informed in the current affairs of both Europe and America. Using his practical insight to establish towns, his inherited ships to establish trade, and his Biblical convictions to establish truth in the land, Francis Makemie became the most influential Presbyterian preacher in Maryland and Virginia. He was the "Father of American Presbyterianism."

Arrest and Trial in Virginia

In 1689 the English Parliament passed the Toleration Act, affording some degree of religious liberty in the land. In 1692, however, the Church of England became the established church in Maryland. Like Virginia, Maryland laws now required "dissenting" churches, such as Makemie's, to obtain special permits and compelled everyone to pay a special tax to support the clergy of the Church of England. In Virginia the government denied "dissenters" the right to use church buildings. Dissenters met for worship only in their own homes. Finally, in 1699 the Virginia authorities arrested Francis Makemie for preaching without a government license and brought him before the Council at Williamsburg.

Appearing as his own defense before the governor and burgesses, Makemie declared that he was a loyal citizen of "Her Excellency's Ancient and Noble Colony of Virginia: Laboring continuously to propagate the true knowledge of the Christian Religion, and to encourage the strictest justice of all Judicature.'' He argued that the Act of Toleration was in force in the colonies as well as in England. Under English Common Law, argued Makemie, ''an Englishman's house is his castle.'' Surely a person has the right to worship with his friends in his own home.

So satisfactorily did Francis Makemie plead his case that the governor not only licensed his dwelling in Onancock, Virginia, as a ''preaching post,'' but he also permitted Makemie to preach anywhere in the colony. This was an unprecedented concession to ''dissenters.'' Through Makemie's influence, the Virginia General Assembly affirmed on April 16, 1699, that the Act of Toleration was the law of Virginia. This was only the beginning of that long and costly struggle for the religious freedom which America now enjoys.

Arrest and Trial in New York

The deputy governor of New York and New Jersey at this time was Lord Cornbury, the grandson of the earl of Clarendon and first cousin of Queens Mary II and Anne. Symbolic of all that was corrupt in colonial rule, Cornbury illegally disrupted good churches, claiming that only the Church of England was legal.

In January 1707 Francis Makemie and a preacher friend, John Hampton, stopped in New York City on their way to New England. Hearing of Makemie's visit, the Dutch and French Reformed churches asked Cornbury (who was actually entertaining Makemie and Hampton in his own home) for permission for Makemie to preach in their churches. Cornbury refused.

Unaware of these proceedings, Makemie honored the request of Christian friends in the city to preach in the Pearl Street home of William Jackson, a local shoemaker, on Sunday, January 19. About ten persons attended. On Wednesday Cornbury issued a warrant for Makemie's arrest in Long Island. The authorities brought the preacher to Fort Anne to face the governor himself.

''How dare you to take upon you to preach in my government without my license?'' demanded Cornbury. In vain Makemie strived to convince the governor that the Act of Toleration gave him liberty to preach ''in any of Her Majesty's dominions.'' To this Cornbury responded, ''You shall not spread your pernicious doctrines here.'' He then demanded that Makemie give ''bonds and security'' to assure his ''good behavior'' and to assure that he would not preach anymore under Cornbury's government. To this the staunch Scotch-Irishman stood ready to respond.

''Endeavoring always so to live as to keep a conscience void of offense towards God and man . . . we would give security for our behavior,'' explained the preacher, ''but to give bond and security to preach no more in your Excellency's government, if invited and desired by any people, *we neither can nor dare do.*''

''Then you must go to jail,'' retorted Cornbury. He then charged Makemie for preaching in an assembly of more than five persons without a license and placed him in prison to await a trial, which was not scheduled to occur until the following June. While in prison Makemie prepared for publication the sermon called *A Good Conversation,* which he had preached in the shoemaker's home. After more than six weeks, Makemie applied to the Supreme Court on writ of *habeas corpus.* The authorities released him on bail on March 11, 1707.

Makemie returned to New York in June to stand trial. Three of the ablest lawyers in the province defended him, but when they had concluded their arguments, Makemie arose and spoke in his own defense. With great force of argument, the preacher vindicated himself from every charge and proved more than a match for the prosecuting attorney. He demonstrated unusual familiarity with English law.

Finally, on June 7, after a long and sensational trial, the chief justice of the court ordered that Francis Makemie be acquitted on the grounds that he had complied with the conditions of the Toleration Act. Thus his license, originally issued in Barbados and recognized in Virginia and Maryland, was now officially valid throughout the queen's domain. The court, however, required Makemie to pay his own trial expense of over £83—an amount which exceeded the yearly salary of most dissenting preachers.

The unreasonable court expenses so aroused the citizenry that the following year the New York Assembly passed an act making illegal the assessing of an innocent party for his trial expenses. As for Cornbury, his tyranny in the Makemie affair was the major cause for his own imprisonment and disgraceful recall as governor. Defending himself in a letter to the Lords of Trade, Cornbury described Makemie as a ''Jack of all Trades: he is a preacher, a Doctor of Physick, a Merchant, an Attorney, or Counsellor at Law, and, which is worse of all, a Disturber of Governments.''

Francis Makemie died only a year after his trial. He had literally worn himself out for the cause of righteousness.

Suggestions for Further Reading

Boyd S. Schlenther. *The Life and Writings of Francis Makemie.* Philadelphia: Presbyterian Historical Society, 1971. [Contains a fifteen-page sketch of the life of Makemie and Makemie's extant short writings and letters]

The Great Awakening

Jonathan Edwards:
America's Theologian-Preacher

by Edward M. Panosian

Jonathan Edwards is probably the best-known figure associated with the Great Awakening. He has often been caricatured, however, simply as the "fire-and-brimstone" preacher of "Sinners in the Hands of an Angry God." Indeed, some secular writers, embarrassed by this distortion, have even attempted to reverse that picture completely, portraying a brilliant New England thinker who was only incidentally religious. The truth is that Edwards was a multifaceted man—certainly brilliant and undeniably a keen logician, but also an intensely religious man of deep and reverent piety. It is Jonathan Edwards, perhaps, not philosopher Baruch Spinoza, who deserves the description "the God-intoxicated man."

Preacher, scholar, missionary, philosopher, father, theologian, and saint—these were the earthly roles of Jonathan Edwards. Gentle, firm, industrious, serious, profound, disciplined, and balanced—these were his most compelling characteristics. He was a man of character, involved in controversy, a man who no less now than during his life evokes the praise of brethren and the calumny of foes.

He was called to live during a time of difficult transition, from the colonial to the revolutionary period. In the distance behind him were the fading memories of the pious days of Pilgrim and Puritan; in the distance ahead, the anticipation of secular society, "enlightenment" religion, and separation of church and state. While he sought to renew what was, he sharpened the contrast with what was to come.

Born in 1703, just three months after John Wesley and an ocean apart, the only son among the eleven children of the Reverend Timothy and Esther Edwards, in the parish of East Windsor, Connecticut, with ministers and merchants in his heritage on both sides, this lad, who was to grow to become the foremost theologian of early America, gave early promise of his difference from his peers. As a child he was docile, reflective, affectionate, and sensitive, but, above all, precocious. His intellectual activity was remarkable. He began then what was to be his practice throughout life: writing to cultivate thought.

From Edwards's pen, when his fingers were but twelve and thirteen years old, came such essays as one, of a thousand words, on the habits of the field spider. Another was an analysis of colors and the rainbow. Another was a demonstration that the soul is not material. If these seem strange subjects for such tender youth, they reflect something of the uniqueness of this fertile mind and its uncommon thirst for knowledge.

That thirst, perhaps first cultivated by the elementary schooling provided him by his father, respected as minister and teacher, was furthered by the lad's entry at Yale College in 1716, just before his thirteenth birthday. Here he took the established course of ministerial training, read Locke and Newton, wrote essays on Berkeley's philosophy, yet reflected little participation in typical nonacademic activities of college life. Never outgoing or given easily to social graces, little able to enjoy the frivolous or the vain, he seemed aloof from his fellows. Because he served as college butler in his senior year, one who ladled out the meat and potatoes at mealtime, he enjoyed little society even at meals.

Having completed the course in 1720, a Yale graduate at seventeen, he remained for further study before taking a Presbyterian pulpit briefly in New York in 1722. Even more briefly he preached in Bolton, Connecticut, before being invited back to Yale to take the master's degree, to serve as tutor, and to perform administrative duties during an interlude of several months when there was no president.

It was during these years between graduation and his being "settled" in the Northampton parish which became inextricably linked with his name that Jonathan Edwards was converted, enjoyed that "sweet delight in God and divine things," and set down in his diary a covenant and a determination to dedicate all his effort to the service of God. As he read Paul's First Epistle to Timothy, there struck most deeply to his soul verse 17 of chapter one: "Now unto the King eternal, immortal, invisible, the only wise God, be honour and glory for ever and ever. Amen."

Inexplicably, this verse, so atypical of verses which are often used of the Holy Spirit to strike conviction and convert hearts, caused the young man's soul to be turned to the realization of who God is and His claim on the total being of man. This depth of understanding and solemnity of purpose was typical of this philosopher-genius who was equally soulwinning preacher. In his own words,

As I read the words, there came into my soul . . . a sense of the glory of the Divine Being; a new sense, quite different from any thing I ever experienced before. Never any words of Scripture seemed to me as these words did. I thought with myself, how excellent a Being that was, and how happy I should be, if I might enjoy that God, and be rapt up to Him in Heaven, and be as it were swallowed up in him for ever! . . . From about that time, I began to have a new kind of apprehension . . . of Christ, and the work of redemption, and the glorious way of salvation by Him. An inward, sweet sense of these things . . . came into my heart.

Not long afterward, his diary and notebooks of meditations reflect the resolutions of his will in the service of Christ. Particularly beginning in January of 1723, and continuing through the spring and summer of that year are such revealing entries as these:

Now, henceforth, I am not to act, in any respect, as my own. I shall act as my own, if I ever make use of any of my powers, to any thing, that is not to the glory of God, and do not make the glorying of Him, my whole and entire business; if I murmur in the least at affliction; if I grieve at the prosperity of others; if I am in any way uncharitable; if I am angry, because of injuries; if I revenge them; if I do any thing, purely to please myself, or if I avoid any thing, for the sake of my own ease; if I omit any thing, because it is great denial; if I trust to myself, if I take any of the praise of any good that I do, or that God doth by me; or if I am in any way proud.

* * *

Resolved, that no other end but religion, shall have any influence at all on any of my actions; and that no action shall be, in the least circumstance, any otherwise than the religious end will carry it.

* * *

Never let me trifle with a book with which I may have no present concern.

These samples, of so many others like them, reflect the dedication and singleness of mind and heart of the man of twenty-three who was called as colleague pastor to his maternal grandfather, the Reverend Solomon Stoddard, at Northampton, Massachusetts, in November of 1726. Here he was to labor in that service and devotion for almost the quarter century that followed.

Northampton was the most important inland city in New England, ecclesiastically second only to Boston. The congregation had sought a likely successor to the aging Mr. Stoddard, who had been pastor over fifty years. More than one generation had grown up knowing only him as pastor. Edwards came with high expectations.

Faith of Our Fathers: Scenes from American Church History

Not long after his coming, he married, when she was seventeen, Sarah Pierrepont, daughter of the minister of New Haven, great-granddaughter of Thomas Hooker, combining in that marriage three very illustrious families. Edwards described her as "of a wonderful sweetness, calmness and universal benevolence of mind." Reared in her father's parsonage, she was easily able to make of her husband's a place of singular and practical piety. Both a Mary and a Martha, she did much serving and caring for the material needs of a growing family (there were eleven children in all); she was also meditative and spiritual, a woman of deep feeling.

With the death of Stoddard two years after Edwards was ordained to succeed him, the younger now assumed all the responsibilities of the parish. He was twenty-six. More preacher and teacher than pastor, he regularly spent thirteen hours daily in his study. His practice was to rise at four A.M. (at five in winter). He carefully regulated his diet, eating what could be easily and quickly digested, so that his mind would remain most active. For exercise he chopped wood or rode horseback. Ever eager to "improve his time," on long rides he would take pins and little pieces of paper; whenever he had an idea he wished to remember, he would pin a paper to his coat to remind him, after the ride, to write down the idea.

The pulpit was his throne. Jonathan Edwards gave most of his mental and physical energy to the preparing and delivering of sermons. We possess today manuscripts or outlines for about a thousand of these. He preached on Sunday (usually for two hours) and gave the teaching lecture on Thursday. To his congregation of about six hundred, he would usually read (from the small booklet he had made by sewing together small pieces of paper, 3 7/8 by 4 1/8 inches, most of which had been used for other purposes on the other side—a picture of his native frugality, of things no less than time) the closely reasoned exposition in the Puritan style.

Each sermon was begun with the assertion of a subject, "the doctrine"; next came the series of developed points, "the reasons, or proofs"; finally, the applications or "uses." The text was often not immediately obvious and usually an unfamiliar one, but wonderfully replete with the "doctrine" he was presenting. His best known sermon, for example—"Sinners in the Hands of an Angry God"—developed an almost unknown text: "Their foot shall slide in due time" (Deut. 32:35).

And his people listened. His voice was not strong, but solemn and distinct. He possessed a quiet intensity, "looking and speaking as in the presence of God." He was deliberate and piercing. He spoke less a series of words than a message. His was the eloquence that moves to action after the words are forgotten.

Contributing to his later difficulties with his people was his preference for his study over their society. He believed he could do more good for his people by writing and preaching, catechizing the children in small groups, and counseling his people in his study, than by visiting in their homes. Some interpreted this practice, so in contrast with the late Mr. Stoddard, as an aloofness, rather than his natural reticence. Physically frail most of his life, Edwards conserved his energy for what he believed was its most profitable use. Yet he always went to his people when sent for, to the sick and to the afflicted. And ministers and other dignitaries, when passing through, found—and often later wrote of—his cordial hospitality and gracious care and provision for their welfare. George Whitefield was one such.

Whitefield reminds of the renewal of the Great Awakening in New England. Earlier, in the last months of 1734, a series of sermons Edwards preached in his parish was followed by several sudden and violent conversions, particularly of individuals known to be notorious sinners. That winter and spring a genuine revival broke out in Northampton, with perhaps three hundred saved. Strife, backbiting, and gossiping subsided among the people. Almost as quickly as it had begun, the revival ended by May and June. For the next several years Edwards sought to revive the spirit of 1735.

By the 1740s the Awakening, part of a movement which had begun simultaneously in the middle colonies, was again reaping a harvest of souls in New England. Whitefield was helping to spread it as well. Never primarily an itinerant like Whitefield, Edwards was occasionally invited to preach at other parishes. In this context he preached the sermon so blessed at Enfield, Connecticut, in 1741, "Sinners in the Hands of an Angry God." God honored it mightily.

Because of emotional and physical excesses accompanying some of the Awakening, Edwards, by a series of writings and by his preaching, counseled moderation and balance of the head and the heart. Aware of excesses and "false fire," he suggested ways of distinguishing false from true conversions. Among his significant works in the 1730s and 1740s are these, their titles clearly proclaiming their content: *A Faithful Narrative of the Surprising Work of God; The Distinguishing Marks of God; The Distinguishing Marks of a Work of the Spirit of God; Personal Narrative; Some Thoughts Concerning the Present Revival in New England;* and *A Treatise Concerning Religious Affections.*

But for Jonathan Edwards, as minister at Northampton, the tide was turning and the sands were running out. In 1744 he had made a number of enemies by refusing to compromise his beliefs on church discipline when a group of young people were discovered reading and exchanging "lascivious and obscene" books, probably manuals for midwives. Although the congregation agreed the matter should be investigated, when their pastor read publicly a list of names of those he wished to interrogate—unwisely not distinguishing between witnesses and accused—the congregation was inflamed. Too many sons of too many families of prominence were included in the yet indiscriminate list. This attitude made bolder the insolence of the guilty and left embers to smolder long after the fire had subsided.

In the interlude before the final conflict, the Edwards home experienced a grievous event. The young missionary to the American Indians, David Brainerd, betrothed to Jonathan and Sarah's daughter Jerusha, died in their home after several months of nursing the body which had been wasted for several years by tuberculosis. Jerusha herself followed her beloved David in death after just four months.

Two brief chapters remain. The first is Edwards's dismissal from Northampton. The issue was joined in 1749 and consummated in June of 1750. Edwards, after more than twenty years of concurrence, concluded that "Stoddard's Way" was wrong. Stoddard had gone beyond the "Half-Way Covenant" of 1662 (which had permitted a "half-way" church membership for those baptized as infants but who had never "owned the covenant," given evidence or an account of conversion). Although these "half-way" members had been denied access to the Lord's Supper, as unconverted church members, Stoddard had further permitted them to participate in that ordinance, giving them all the privileges of believers, as long as they were not "openly scandalous" in their way of life.

While we may wonder at his tardiness in doing so, Pastor Edwards, in seeking to restore stricter definitions for church members, published his "Qualifications for Full Communion," demanding examination of the *heart* condition of those who presented themselves as members. This was nothing more than separating chaff from wheat, sheep from acknowledged goats. But the obscene books episode and the apparent aloofness of their pastor joined now with this new resentment to cause the camel, whose head had been allowed in the tent, to expel the tent chief. In 1750, after twenty-three years as their pastor, at age forty-seven, with eight children at home, Jonathan Edwards was turned out of the pastorate of his lifetime, unpracticed in the ways of the world, but dependent on the will of heaven.

The last chapter is the fruitful harvest at Stockbridge, sixty miles away. Here Edwards was called to be a pastor to a small flock and missionary to the Housatunnock Indians. Twelve white families and 250 Indian families made up the population. Not well-fitted for such a role, yet isolated still farther from the bustle of the world, he was given now of God the opportunity to reap with his pen the harvest of decades of sowing of seed thoughts. It was here at Stockbridge that he wrote works on the freedom of the will, on the nature of virtue, and on original sin, for which he is chiefly noted.

Finally, in 1757, Jonathan Edwards was called to be president of the College of New Jersey, which had moved to and was eventually to be known as Princeton. However, this apparent earthly honor, a fitting recognition of his singular and pious gifts—in a day when Princeton was known for such virtues—was not to be. He arrived in February of 1758 and was installed as president. There had been a serious epidemic of smallpox in neighboring towns. It was sensible to be inoculated, and so was the new president a week later. A month later he was dead.

He had finished a course and left a heritage of submission to the God who doeth all things well. Whatever and wherever in his life change had come, his will had been actively resigned to the will of God. He stood for "heart religion." He delighted in the "sweet things of religion," and in his life he sought to live to the honor and glory of "the King eternal, immortal, invisible, the only wise God." When shall we see another?

Suggestions for Further Reading

Keith J. Hardman. *The Spiritual Awakeners*. Chicago: Moody Press, 1983. [See pp. 61-73.]

"Jonathan Edwards and the Great Awakening." *Christian History,* vol. 4, no. 4 (1985). [Entire issue]

Iain H. Murray. *Jonathan Edwards: A New Biography*. Edinburgh: Banner of Truth Trust, 1987.

The Log College

by David O. Beale

Next to Jonathan Edwards, the leading American preacher of the Great Awakening was Gilbert Tennent of Pennsylvania. Tennent was a man of unusual abilities, but part of the credit for his accomplishments—humanly speaking—must go to the unusual education that he, his brothers, and several others received from Gilbert's father, William Tennent, Sr. Their "log college" may not have been an Ivy League school, but it certainly was—as George Whitefield called it—a "school of the prophets."

William Tennent, Sr., middle-aged Scotch-Irishman, sailed from Northern Ireland to America about 1718 with his wife and children. Soon after landing at Philadelphia, he settled into his life-pastorate, the Neshaminy Presbyterian Church in Bucks County, Pennsylvania. It was here that Mr. Tennent resolved to establish a school to educate his four sons for the ministry. Nine additional students brought the original enrollment to thirteen. Before then, no young man could enter the Presbyterian ministry without traveling to New England or even to Scotland for his education.

During the first few months, the students boarded at nearby farms or lived in the Tennent household where Mrs. Tennent tried to give them the necessary "mothering." Tennent soon erected a humble log building within a few steps of his parsonage. Some of this small group of dedicated young men moved into the crude attic above the single classroom and cooked their meals in the open fireplace. The students' day began in prayer at 5:00 A.M. and concluded with bedtime at 9:00 P.M., after a full day of class instruction. They attended the Neshaminy church on Sundays. Like every good work, however, the little college had its enemies. Critics who had grown accustomed to the European universities' handsome stone edifices contemptuously referred to Mr. Tennent's school as the "Log College."

William Tennent, Sr.—making the most of the facilities at his disposal—was a well-read theologian, educated at Edinburgh University, as well as a warm and faithful teacher. He was a Greek and Hebrew scholar and could write and speak Latin with perfect ease. Most important, however, he was a pastor of unusual ability and a man of genuine piety and evangelistic zeal. His little "school of the prophets" marked an epoch in the history of ministerial training in America.

When the English evangelist George Whitefield first visited Philadelphia, in 1739, Mr. Tennent traveled twenty miles to the city to enjoy his fellowship. The entry in Mr. Whitefield's diary describes the occasion: "At my return home [from visiting a family] was much comforted by the coming of one Mr. Tennent, an old gray-headed disciple and servant of Jesus Christ [who] keeps an Academy about twenty miles from Philadelphia, and has been blessed with four gracious sons."

On his return from New York, Whitefield visited Neshaminy where he preached to about three thousand people gathered in the "meeting house yard." The Spirit of the Lord blessed the service with a "great melting down" in the hearts of the people. Whitefield, on this occasion, penned a description of the old Tennent school: "The place wherein the young men study now is in contempt called the *college*. It is a Log-House, about twenty feet long, and near as many broad."

All of the thirteen original Log College students became pioneers of Christian education in America, and a number of these young preachers founded educational institutions. A monument at the site of the Log College lists fifty-one colleges which stemmed from this little school. William Tennent, Sr., died in 1746 at the age of seventy-three. The following year the log building closed with the opening of its successor—the College of New Jersey (later named Princeton University).

Dr. Archibald Alexander later observed that a major advantage which the Log College students possessed was that "the spirit of piety seems to have been nourished in that institution with assiduous care. . . . They had, we have reason to believe, the teaching of the Holy Spirit." The major factor which contributed to the school's success in those years was that William Tennent, Sr.'s sons stood faithful to "the cause" for which he himself had so faithfully given his life.

Gilbert Tennent (1703-1764)

Gilbert, the eldest son, came with his family from Ireland when he was fourteen years old. After his log-college training, he tutored at the school for about a year. Struggling for perfect assurance about God's call into the ministry, he studied medicine for a while. Finally, he settled the matter once for all—Gilbert Tennent knew that he must preach the gospel. Yale University conferred an honorary Master of Arts degree upon him in 1725, the same year that the Presbyterian church licensed him to preach. After preaching for a while in Newcastle, Delaware,

Gilbert settled into the pastorate at New Brunswick, New Jersey, and received ordination in 1727.

For at least six months after his coming to New Brunswick, the young pastor did not see a single conversion to Christ. Already distressed and discouraged, he became deathly ill. It was during this crisis that Gilbert promised God that if He would allow him six more months, he would "stand upon the stage of the world, as it were, and plead more faithfully for his cause, and take more earnest pains for the salvation of souls."

Gilbert Tennent kept his promise. The Lord God transformed his health and his ministry, and the preacher ministered with a new sense of urgency. About 1739 at Nottingham, Pennsylvania, he preached one of America's most famous sermons—"The Danger of an Unconverted Ministry." He used Mark 6:34 as his text. Gilbert feared that many pastors—even in that day—were failing to declare the whole counsel of God and that some had never experienced saving grace.

In 1740 George Whitefield persuaded Gilbert to make a preaching tour as far as Boston, to water the good seed which Whitefield himself had sown. Preaching almost every day for three months, Tennent witnessed a spiritual "shaking among the dry bones." Local Boston pastors rejoiced that literally hundreds of concerned souls came to them during this short time to find salvation or assurance. One pastor declared that more had come to him in one week than during his entire twenty-four-year ministry. Gilbert never kept a written account of the number of conversions under his ministry: "I cannot offer any precise conjecture," he remarks, "and shall therefore leave it to be determined at the judgment-day."

In 1743, after sixteen years in his New Brunswick pastorate, Gilbert answered God's call to Philadelphia to serve as pastor of a new work which a dedicated group of Whitefield's converts was establishing.

He considered himself the father of his people, whom he counseled, warned, and reproved with all the tenderness and solicitude of a father's heart. Dr. Samuel Finley said of Gilbert, "Above other things, the purity of the ministry was his care; and . . . he zealously urged every scriptural method, by which carnal and earthly-minded men might be kept from entering into it."

Gilbert Tennent died at the age of sixty-one almost forty years after that despairing day on which he had begged God for just six more months to preach. Those who heard him never forgot that preaching. "Hypocrites must either soon be converted or enraged," wrote George Whitefield of Gilbert's message.

John Tennent (1706-1732)

John, the third son of William Tennent Sr., was twelve when his family came to America. After receiving his training at his father's Log College, he accepted the call to become the pastor of a church near

Freehold, in Monmouth County, New Jersey. After a brief but fruitful ministry, John died of tuberculosis at the age of twenty-five. His brother Gilbert said of him, "He gained more poor sinners to Christ in that little compass of time . . . , about three and a half years, than many in the space of twenty, thirty, forty, or fifty years."

William Tennent, Jr. (1705-1777)

William Tennent, Jr.—born in Ireland—arrived in America with his family when he was thirteen. Early in life, William revealed an uncommon thirst for knowledge. He graduated from his father's Log College, then traveled to New Brunswick to study under his brother Gilbert.

During the laborious preparation for his ministerial examination, at the age of nineteen, William fell sick. He lapsed into a "remarkable trance," which lasted three days. His relatives, thinking that he was dead, were at the point of burying him, when he revived—breaking up his own funeral. William regained his health after about a year, but he had lost all previous learning, including the ability to read and write. After a time, however, his knowledge began rapidly to return.

Upon his brother John's death, William accepted the call to succeed him as pastor of the Old Tennent Church. Students at the College of New Jersey often walked twenty miles to hear him preach. As a trustee of the college, William Tennent, Jr., always kept a watchful eye over the school's spiritual well-being. He once arrived late at a board meeting, to hear his colleagues favorably discussing a proposition from the governor of New Jersey which would revise the college's charter, to place the school under "state" control in exchange for a monetary benefit. After a while, Mr. Tennent rose to his feet and said, "Brethren! are you mad? I say, brethren, are you mad? Rather than accept the offer . . . , I would set fire to the College edifice at its four corners, and run away in the light of the flames." Needless to say, the trustees ended the bargaining.

William faithfully served until his death in 1777. Dr. Elias Boudinot said of him, "His people loved him as a father; revered him as the pastor and bishop of their souls; obeyed him as their instructor; and delighted in his company and private conversation as of a friend and brother."

Princeton Seminary—today a hotbed of liberal and radical theology—has for many years repudiated everything that William Tennent, Sr., and his sons held so dearly. "How are the mighty fallen, and the weapons of war perished!" (II Sam. 1:27).

Suggestions for Further Reading

Archibald Alexander. *The Log College*. 1851. Reprint. Edinburgh: Banner of Truth Trust, 1968.

The Preacher and the Printer

by Rebecca Lunceford Foster

In our overspecialized age, it is easy to forget that men whose lives we study separately—great religious leaders of the past, for instance, and the founding fathers of our country—were contemporaries. They were often at the same places at the same time, sometimes even together as friends. Such was the case with Benjamin Franklin and George Whitefield, the English evangelist who was instrumental in the Great Awakening of the eighteenth century.

Whitefield's preaching in England and America brought thousands of souls to the Saviour. A contemporary of such men as John Wesley and Jonathan Edwards, he spent his life in the service of His Lord. Franklin, on the other hand, spent his life in the service of his country. Like many of his contemporaries, he was a practical Deist, acknowledging the existence of God as Creator and Provider but not recognizing the claims of Jesus Christ as the Saviour of sinful men. Indeed, Franklin's Autobiography *reflects his belief in the perfectibility of man and records his efforts to achieve this perfection.*

Christian and Deist, preacher and printer, glorifier of God and glorifier of the human mind—what had these two men to do with each other? Whitefield visited Franklin's Philadelphia in 1739, and Franklin—always interested in events around him—recorded the occasion in the Autobiography.

In 1739 arrived among us from Ireland the Reverend Mr. Whitefield, who had made himself remarkable there as an itinerant preacher. He was at first permitted to preach in some of our churches; but the clergy taking a dislike to him, soon refus'd him their Pulpits and he was oblig'd to preach in the fields. The multitudes of all sects and denominations that attended his sermons were enormous, and it was matter of speculation to me, who was one of the number, to observe the extraordinary influence of his oratory on his hearers, and how much they admir'd and respected him, notwithstanding his common abuse of them, by assuring them they were naturally *half beasts and half devils.* It was wonderful to see the change soon made in the manners of our inhabitants. From being thoughtless or indifferent about religion, it seem'd as if all the world were growing religious, so that one could not walk thro' the town in an evening without hearing psalms sung in different families of every street. . . .

Mr. Whitefield, in leaving us, went preaching all the way thro' the colonies to Georgia. The settlement of that province had lately been begun, but, instead of being made with hardy, industrious husbandmen accustomed to labour, the only people fit for such an enterprise, it was with the families of broken shop-keepers and other insolvent debtors, many of indolent and idle habits, taken out of the jails, who, being set down in the woods, unqualified for clearing land, and unable to endure the hardships of a new settlement, perished in numbers, leaving many helpless children unprovided for. The sight of their miserable situation inspir'd the benevolent heart of Mr. Whitefield with the Idea of building an Orphan House there, in which they might be supported and educated. Returning northward he preach'd up this charity, and made large collections, for his eloquence had a wonderful power over the hearts and purses of his hearers, of which I myself was an instance.

I did not disapprove of the design, but, as Georgia was then destitute of materials and workmen, and it was propos'd to send them from Philadelphia at a great expense, I thought it would have been better to have built the house here and brought the children to it. This I advis'd; but he was resolute in his first project, rejected my counsel, and I thereupon refus'd to contribute. I happened soon after to attend one of his sermons, in the course of which I perceived he intended to finish with a collection, and I silently resolved he should get nothing from me. I had in my pocket a handful of copper money, three or four silver dollars, and five pistoles in gold. As he proceeded I began to soften, and concluded to give the coppers. Another stroke of his oratory made me asham'd of that, and determin'd me to give the silver; and he finsh'd so admirably, that I empty'd my pocket wholly into the collector's dish, gold and all. At this sermon there was also one of our club, who, being of my sentiments respecting the building in Georgia, and suspecting a collection might be intended, had, by precaution, emptied his pockets before he came from home. Towards the conclusion of the discourse, however, he felt a strong desire to give, and apply'd to a neighbour who stood near him, to borrow some money for the purpose. The application was unfortunately [made] to perhaps the only man in the company who had the firmness not to be affected by the preacher. His answer was, *"At any other time, Friend Hopkinson, I would lend to thee freely; but not now, for thee seems to be out of thy right senses."*

Faith of Our Fathers: Scenes from American Church History

Some of Mr. Whitefield's enemies affected to suppose that he would apply these collections to his own private emolument; but I, who was intimately acquainted with him (being employ'd in printing his Sermons and Journals, etc.), never had the least suspicion of his integrity, but am to this day decidedly of opinion that he was in all his conduct a perfectly *honest man;* and methinks my testimony in his favour ought to have the more weight, as we had no religious connection. He us'd, indeed, sometimes to pray for my conversion, but never had the satisfaction of believing that his prayers were heard. Ours was a mere civil friendship, sincere on both sides, and lasted to his death.

The following instance will show something of the terms on which we stood. Upon one of his arrivals from England at Boston, he wrote to me that he should come soon to Philadelphia, but knew not where he could lodge when there. . . . My answer was, "You know my house; if you can make shift with its scanty accommodations, you will be most heartily welcome." He reply'd, that if I made that kind offer for Christ's sake, I should not miss of a reward. And I returned, *"Don't let me be mistaken; it was not for Christ's sake, but for your sake."* One of our common acquaintance jocosely remark'd, that, knowing it to be the custom of the saints, when they received any favour, to shift the burden of the obligation from off their own shoulders, and place it in heaven, I had contriv'd to fix it on earth. . . .

He had a loud and clear voice, and articulated his words and sentences so perfectly, that he might be heard and understood at a great distance. . . . Without being interested in the subject, one could not help being pleas'd with the discourse; a pleasure of much the same kind with that receiv'd from an excellent piece of musick.

> [*The "intimate acquaintance" between the two men was at least partly carried on by letters in which Whitefield did not hesitate to speak of Franklin's spiritual condition. One letter dealing with business, written in late 1740, closed with these words:*]

Dear sir, adieu! I do not despair of your seeing the reasonableness of Christianity. Apply to God; be willing to do the Divine will, and you shall know it. Oh! the love of God to your unworthy friend.

George Whitefield

> [*Franklin's lack of understanding of the real purposes of Whitefield's ministry is nowhere more apparent than in a letter written July 6, 1749, in which he observed the following:*]

I am glad to hear that you have frequent opportunities of preaching among the great. If you gain them to a good and exemplary life, wonderful changes will follow in the manners of the lower ranks. . . . On this principle, Confucius, the famous eastern reformer, proceeded. When he saw his country sunk in vice, and wickedness of all kinds triumphant, he applied himself first to the grandees; and, having, by his doctrine, won them to the cause of virtue, the commons followed in multitudes. The mode has a wonderful influence on mankind; and there are numbers, who, perhaps, fear less the being in hell, than out of the fashion. Our more western reformations began with the ignorant mob; and, when numbers of them were gained, interest and party-views drew in the wise and great. Where both methods can be used, reformations are likely to be more speedy. O that some method could be found to make them lasting! He who discovers that, will, in my opinion, deserve more, ten thousand times, than the inventor of the longitude.

[His friend, whose concern was not for reformation of lives but regeneration of hearts, wrote to Franklin after the inventor's experiments with electricity.]

London, August 17, 1752

Dear Mr. Franklin,

I find that you grow more and more famous in the learned world. As you have made a pretty considerable progress in the mysteries of electricity, I would now humbly recommend to your diligent unprejudiced pursuit and study the mystery of the new birth. It is a most important, interesting study, and when mastered, will richly repay you for all your pains. One, at whose bar we are shortly to appear, hath solemnly declared, that, without it "we cannot enter into the kingdom of heaven." You will excuse this freedom. I must have *aliquid Christi* [something of Christ] in all my letters.

I am yet a willing pilgrim for His great name's sake, and I trust a blessing attends my poor feeble labours. To the giver of every good gift be all the glory! My respects await yourself and all enquiring friends; and hoping to see you once more in the land of the living, I subscribe myself, dear sir, your very affectionate friend, and obliged servant,

George Whitefield

[In 1756, twenty years before the events of the American Revolution which were to crown Franklin's career, he wrote a letter to Whitefield which reflected his uncertainty about his accomplishments. In part, he wrote:]

Life, like a dramatic piece, should not only be conducted with regularity, but, methinks, it should finish handsomely. Being now in the last act, I begin to cast about for something fit to end it with. Or, if mine be more properly compared to an epigram, as some of its lines are but barely tolerable, I am very desirous of concluding with a bright point.... I thank you for your good wishes and prayers; and am, with the greatest esteem and affection, dear sir, your most obedient humble servant,

Benjamin Franklin

[Soon, the strained relationship between Great Britain and her American colonies resulted in Franklin's being sent to London to negotiate with the government concerning the problems of the colonies. He went first in 1757 and stayed until late 1762 and again from 1764 to 1775. During the second mission, news of the unrest at home caused him to write to Whitefield, in a letter dated early in 1768:]

I am under continued apprehensions that we may have bad news from America. The sending soldiers to Boston always appeared to me a dangerous step; they could do no good, they might occasion mischief. When I consider the warm resentment of a people who think themselves injured and oppressed, and the common insolence of the soldiery who are taught to consider that people as in rebellion, I cannot but fear the consequences of bringing them together. It seems like setting up a smith's forge in a magazine of gunpowder. I *see* with you that our affairs are not well managed by our rulers here below; I wish I could *believe* with you, that they are well attended to by those above; I rather suspect, from certain circumstances, that though the general government of the universe is well administered, our particular little affairs are perhaps below notice, and left to take the chance of human prudence or imprudence, as either may happen to be uppermost. It is, however, an uncomfortable thought, and I leave it.

[The great preacher, reading those words, wrote on the letter]

Uncomfortable indeed! and, blessed be God, *unscriptural;* for we are fully assured that "the Lord reigneth," and are directed to cast *all* our care on Him, because He careth for us.

Franklin's Autobiography *and letters show his perception of Whitefield's influence on others, but they are sadly imperceptive of his own needs and the answer Whitefield taught. Benjamin Franklin heard the Great Awakener's sermons, not as a testimony of God's saving grace, but as an example of great oratory in the interest of human reformation. His friend's witness and prayers for Franklin's salvation did not move the influential printer, inventor, and philosopher to repentance, even though Franklin sought for proof of meaning and guidance in the universe. If they had, we can only wonder what might have been the effect on the Great Awakening and American history.*

Suggestions for Further Reading

Benjamin Franklin. *Autobiography.* [Available in several editions]

Arnold Dallimore. *George Whitefield.* Westchester, Ill.: Crossway Books, 1990. [Abridged by the author from his larger two-volume biography of Whitefield]

Keith J. Hardman. *The Spiritual Awakeners.* Chicago: Moody Press, 1983. [See pp. 75-92.]

Edward M. Panosian. "George Whitefield: The Awakener." In *Faith of Our Fathers: Scenes from Church History,* edited by Mark Sidwell, pp. 145-49. Greenville, S.C.: Bob Jones University Press, 1989.

The Sandy Creek Revival:
The South's Great Awakening

by Mark Sidwell

Most accounts of the Great Awakening focus predominantly on the revivals in the middle colonies and particularly in New England. The South was the scene of revival too, however. Whitefield preached in southern cities, and Presbyterian Samuel Davies led a notable awakening in Virginia. Even farther south, in the Carolinas, was another phase of the Great Awakening, the Sandy Creek Revival.

"A surprising work of God" Jonathan Edwards called the Great Awakening. In the early 1700s the moving of God's Spirit touched, convicted, and converted thousands of Americans. The Reformed denominations (Presbyterian, Congregationalist, and Dutch Reformed) found themselves swept along in a mighty outpouring of God's saving grace. Probably most Christians are at least generally familiar with this "surprising work," but many are unaware of another phase of that same revival. This other phase occurred not in the North, but in the South; not among the Reformed groups of New England, but among the Sandy Creek Baptists of North Carolina.

The man responsible for carrying the fervor of the Great Awakening to the South, Shubal Stearns, was among those influenced by George Whitefield, the powerful English evangelist of the Great Awakening. Stearns was born in Boston in 1706. After his conversion to Christ around 1740, he eventually became a minister with the Baptists. In 1754 God called Stearns from his home in Connecticut to fields farther south. He labored for a short time in Virginia, then moved to Sandy Creek, North Carolina.

North Carolina's piedmont area in the middle of the eighteenth century was part of America's wild frontier. The people were usually irreligious and coarse, and marriages often little more than informal agreements. Backwoods North Carolina was a spiritual as well as a

The Sandy Creek Revival: The South's Great Awakening

physical wilderness, and into this religiously barren land came Stearns and his family.

The small church at Sandy Creek began with sixteen members, half of whom were Stearns's own family. Then the New England minister began to preach, and God's Spirit began to move in North Carolina as He had in Massachusetts. Eighteenth-century Baptist historian Morgan Edwards described Stearns as a man and a preacher:

> Mr. Stearns was but a little man, but of good natural parts, and sound judgment. Of learning he had but a small share, yet was pretty well acquainted with books. His voice was musical and strong, which he managed in such a manner, as one while to make soft impressions on the heart . . . and anon to shake the nerves, and to throw the animal system into tumults and perturbations. His character was indisputably good, both as a man, a Christian, and a preacher.

A noted characteristic of Shubal Stearns was his penetrating gaze. One man, Tidance Lane, described Stearns's influence: "He fixed his eyes upon me immediately," he said, "which made me feel in such a manner as I never felt before." Burdened with conviction, Lane sought relief in walking around, trying to leave, and even shaking hands with the preacher, but all was in vain. When Stearns finally began to preach, Lane's resistance collapsed, and he was converted.

Another story, that of Elnathan Davis, illustrates the convicting power of Stearns's preaching. Davis and some of his rough friends attended a baptism conducted by Stearns. Their interest was hardly spiritual; the subject of baptism was a very large man, while the preacher was rather small; so the idlers half-expected and hoped to see one or the other drown. As Davis drew near, he heard the little minister preaching, and he fell under conviction. He fled back to his companions and said, "There is a trembling and crying spirit among them, but whether it be the spirit of God or the devil I don't know; if it be the devil, the devil go with them, for I will never more venture myself among them!" His resolve melted, however, as God worked in his heart. Davis returned to the preaching, eventually was converted, and later replaced Stearns, after the latter's death, as the most influential minister in the Sandy Creek region.

The work in North Carolina prospered. In a short time, the Sandy Creek church swelled from sixteen members to over six hundred. The "super-churches" of our day diminish for us the impact of this growth, but consider that in the 1700s there were no modern means of transportation or good roads. The people were not concentrated in large cities, but were scattered over the countryside, having to travel difficult miles to attend services. Nor was the Sandy Creek church's impact limited to its own members. Regarding its influence, Morgan Edwards wrote:

> From this Zion went forth the word, and great was the company of them that published it; it . . . had spread branches westward as far as the great river Mississippi; southward as far as Georgia; eastward to the sea and Chesapeake Bay; and northward to the waters of the Potomac; it . . . is become the mother, grandmother, and great-grandmother to 42 churches from which sprang 125 ministers.

The churches that grew out of Stearns's ministry banded together in 1758 as the Sandy Creek Baptist Association. This group, under Stearns's benevolent but firm leadership, sought to advance God's work throughout the southern colonies. Association meetings were marked by prayer, fasting, and exhortation. Aflame with revival, the churches in the association continued to increase in number and influence.

By 1770, however, the association had grown too large and had spread over too great an area to maintain a united, concerted effort. In that year the group divided into three separate associations, one each for North Carolina, South Carolina, and Virginia. The following year Shubal Stearns, the great patriarch of the movement, died and was buried near the meetinghouse in which he had preached. Within a few years Stearns's church had dropped in attendance to a level below that with which it had started. The Awakening ended, but the story did not.

Subsequent history has justified Morgan Edwards's appraisal of the importance of the Sandy Creek Baptist Church. The Sandy Creek Awakening was one of the first revivals in America's South. During the revival souls were saved, lives changed, and perhaps even history shaped. A rich and godly heritage belongs to a small church in the Carolina backwoods.

Suggestions for Further Reading

William L. Lumpkin. *Baptist Foundations in the South.* Nashville: Broadman, 1961.

H. Leon McBeth. *The Baptist Heritage: Four Centuries of Baptist Witness.* Nashville: Broadman, 1987. [Pages 200-251 trace the history of Baptists in the Great Awakening; pages 227-32 concern Sandy Creek in particular.]

George W. Purefoy. *A History of the Sandy Creek Baptist Association.* 1859. Reprint. New York: Arno Press, 1980.

The Early National Era

(1776 to 1865)

The early national era of the United States (1776-1865) began and ended with a revival. The revival that opened the era was the Second Great Awakening, an effusion of God's Spirit that may have surpassed even the first awakening in its impact. In the eastern United States, the revival moved with quiet but profound power in the colleges and churches. Timothy Dwight, president of Yale and grandson of Jonathan Edwards, perhaps typified the eastern revivals. He met scoffers in open debate concerning the truth of Scripture and preached a series of chapel sermons on the fundamentals of Christian theology. The result was a series of revivals within the halls of Yale.

In the West the revival was somewhat noisier but just as dramatic in its results. The Methodists, whose growth in the United States had previously been slowed by John Wesley's opposition to the American Revolution, came into their own in this period. They developed one institution (the circuit rider) and adopted another (the camp meeting) that became the major vehicles of promoting the revival in the West.

The revival touched even foreign lands as it launched America's first great foreign missions movement. In 1806 five students at Williams College in Massachusetts were meeting outdoors for a prayer meeting when a sudden thunderstorm roared up. The group took shelter under a nearby haystack. As they waited out the storm, they talked over how people in foreign fields needed someone to bring them the gospel. One student, Samuel J. Mills, suddenly asked, "Why should *we* not be the ones?" Then he added, *"We can do it if we will!"* Inspired by this "Haystack Prayer Meeting," Mills eventually led the Congregationalists to form the American Board of Commissioners for Foreign Missions, America's first foreign missions board. Soon the ABCFM was sending out missionaries around the world, and other missionaries and denominations joined the effort, such as Adoniram Judson and the Baptists.

American churches also faced numerous challenges in the era between the Revolution and the Civil War. Cults, groups which call themselves Christian but are unorthodox in doctrine, flourished in this era. Probably the most famous were the Mormons, founded by Joseph Smith in 1830. Arousing controversy by their teachings—particularly their practice of polygamy—the group eventually trekked west under the leadership of Brigham Young, where they founded what became the state of Utah. Cults, however, were for the most part outside the church. Of more immediate concern to the churches was an issue that tore at their inner unity—the conflict over slavery. As the controversy between the Northern and Southern sections of the United States heated up, the existence of slavery in the South became a sore point of contention. Northerners roundly condemned slavery; some Southerners, stung by Northern criticism, actually went to the extreme of defending slavery as a "positive good" that improved the quality of life in the South. Other Southerners admitted the evils of slavery but could offer no workable solution for eliminating it without creating tremendous social and economic upheavel in the South. Christians, for the most part, adopted the views of their respective regions toward slavery. A Baptist group in Maine declared, "Of all the systems of iniquity that ever cursed the world, the slave system is the most abominable." A leading South Carolina Baptist, however, claimed that "the right of holding slaves is clearly established in the Holy Scriptures both by precept and example." Most American denominations experienced at least some division over this issue, and in 1844 both the Methodists and the Baptists actually split along North-South lines over slavery.

It would be a mistake, however, to discuss American Christianity only in terms of religious controversies, denominations, and preachers. American society and culture has always borne the stamp of Christians and the contributions they have made. The section "Christians Building a Nation" marks the contributions of soldiers (Robert E. Lee), explorers (Jedediah Strong Smith), scholars (Noah Webster), inventors (Samuel F.B. Morse), and missionaries (the Whitmans). It displays the impact of Christianity on the United States, how Christianity was part of the warp and woof of the very fabric of society.

The period closes with the bloody clash of armies in the American Civil War (1861-1865), a traumatic event that drastically reshaped the course of United States history. Yet prefacing that dark period was America's "Third Great Awakening," the Prayer Meeting Revival. And even in the midst of the horrors of war was the moving of God's Spirit among the soldiers of both armies. Christian faith helped sustain America in one of its greatest hours of trial.

Suggestions for Further Reading

Keith J. Hardman. "The Return of the Spirit: The Second Great Awakening." *Christian History,* vol. 8, no. 3 (1989), pp. 24-31.

The Early National Era (1776 to 1865)

J. Williams Jones. *Christ in the Camp.* 1887. Reprint. Harrisonburg, Va.: Sprinkle Publications, 1986. [On the history of the revivals in the Confederate army]

Peter Marshall and David Manuel. *From Sea to Shining Sea.* Old Tappan, N.J.: Revell, 1985. [Covers the period from 1787 to the Battle of the Alamo (1836)]

Perry Miller. *Life of the Mind in America.* New York: Harcourt, Brace & World, 1965.

Timothy L. Smith. *Revivalism and Social Reform.* New York: Abingdon, 1957.

Bernard A. Weisberger. *They Gathered at the River.* Boston: Little, Brown and Company, 1958. [See pp. 3-159 for a survey of the Second Great Awakening that is entertaining but, unfortunately, somewhat cynical in tone.]

The Second Great Awakening

Asahel Nettleton and the Eastern Revivals

by Mark Sidwell

Christians who are acquainted with the Second Great Awakening tend to associate it with camp meetings and the boisterous revivals of the West. The awakening began in the East, however, where it spread much more quietly among the schools and churches. For instance, President Timothy Dwight of Yale, the grandson of Jonathan Edwards, brought a spirit of Christian devotion to that school which eventually blossomed into a series of revivals among the student body. The most famous evangelist to emerge from the Second Great Awakening was Charles Finney. More typical of the eastern revivals in methodology and theology, however, was one of the beneficiaries of the Yale revivals, Evangelist Asahel Nettleton.

When Evangelist Asahel Nettleton came to Jamaica, Long Island, New York, to hold services in 1826, an elderly believer named Othniel Smith told an acquaintance, "This Mr. Nettleton that is going to preach for us is a most wonderful man; he is said to be the greatest preacher that has been among us since the days of George Whitefield." Mr. Smith would have known; he had heard Whitefield preach when Smith was a young man. Yet today this evangelist who was compared so favorably to Whitefield is rarely mentioned and little known. Who was he to merit such praise?

Asahel Nettleton was born in North Killingworth, Connecticut, in 1783. A member of a nominally religious family, Nettleton gave little thought to God until he was in his late teens. He recalled that his first serious thoughts about life and death came one evening as he watched the sun set and meditated on the fact that one day he would die. The young man soon began a long struggle with a burden of sin. He sought relief in reading the Bible, attending church, and praying as he wandered in the fields or lay in bed at night. Finally, in 1801, he was converted during a revival at Killingworth.

After his conversion, Nettleton wondered whether God wanted him to be something more than a farmer, as the rest of his family had been. Stirred by articles describing foreign mission work, he determined to become a missionary. He saved his money for three years until, in 1805, he was able to enroll at Yale University. Nettleton made only an average record as a student, but he read deeply in theology and was spiritually refreshed and strengthened by a revival that broke out during the 1807-1808 school year.

After graduation Nettleton studied under a pastor in Milford, Connecticut, while he pondered God's will for his life. His change from the mission field to the field of evangelism resulted almost accidentally from the discovery of his spiritual gifts. In 1812 he accepted an invitation to preach in New York. On his way there he stopped to preach in a special service for a pastor in South Britain, Connecticut. To the surprise of all present—including Nettleton—the services launched an awakening in the town, resulting in numerous conversions. Nettleton began preaching in other churches, with equally remarkable results. Friends urged him to consider evangelism as God's calling, pointing to his obvious display of the gifts for that field.

From 1812 to 1822 Nettleton was the nation's leading evangelist, although he preached almost entirely in New England and New York. For the most part, Nettleton's evangelistic work was not so much as a traveling (or ''itinerant'') evangelist but more as a supply preacher in pastorless, spiritually dead churches. In each case he was able to restore the congregations to spiritual ''health'' through the clear and careful preaching of God's Word. Then, his work done, he unobtrusively moved on to another locale.

Caution was the key to his methodology as an evangelist. His preaching was restrained but contained a strong undercurrent of urgency as he confronted sinners with their fate. At times his compassion would burst forth in a stream of eloquent pleading: ''By the mercies of God, and by the terrors of His wrath—by the joys of heaven and pains of hell—by the merits of a Saviour's blood, and by the worth of your immortal souls, I beseech you, lay down the arms of your rebellion; bow and submit to your rightful Sovereign.'' The evangelist always insisted on calm and quiet in his meetings. ''On one occasion,'' wrote his friend Bennet Tyler, ''an individual was so overwhelmed that he lost his self-possession and had begun to make some wild external demonstrations of distress: Dr. N. stopped in the midst of his address, until the person was removed from the room, and then went on, as if nothing unusual had happened.''

Asahel Nettleton and the Eastern Revivals

Nettleton counseled with sinners under conviction both privately and in special "inquiry meetings" held in the church or some rented hall. Nettleton describes one such meeting:

> This evening will never be forgotten. The scene is beyond descrip-tion. Did you ever witness two hundred sinners, with one accord in one place, weeping for their sins? Until you have seen this, you have no adequate conceptions of the solemn scene. I felt as though I was standing on the verge of the eternal world; while the floor under my feet was shaken by the trembling of anxious souls in view of a judgment to come. The solemnity was still heightened, when every knee was bent at the throne of grace, and the inter-vening silence of the voice of prayer was interrupted only by the sighs and sobs of anxious souls.

When dealing privately with an individual, often in the person's home, Nettleton would talk and pray with him at great length. Always he wanted to be sure that a convert understood what he was doing and was not being pressured into some kind of "quick decision." "If other evangelists hit upon the potency of mass evangelism," notes one his-torian, "Nettleton's discovery was the efficacy of the personal approach after the meeting."

The evangelist was concerned, one might even say fearful, that his hearers might not give all credit and glory for the revivals to God. At times this fear led Nettleton, as a modern biographer describes it, to "do his patented disappearing act." Quietly, often without telling any-one, he would leave town. Some congregations were not aware he was gone until they showed up for a service and the preacher did not. This eccentric method often succeeded in shocking churches out of their self-sufficiency, but it caused some misunderstanding as well.

Concerned with the place of music in worship and revival, the evangelist compiled *Village Hymns,* one of the earliest major hymnals in the United States. Through this work Nettleton introduced to the Church such hymns as William Tappan's "'Tis Midnight; and on Olive's Brow" and Samuel Davies' "Great God of Wonders." Sales of this volume were brisk, and the royalties proved large enough to support the evangelist during his latter years and to enable him to endow a theological seminary after his death.

In October 1822 Nettleton became seriously ill with typhus. The sickness was made doubly painful when the friend who nursed the evangelist also fell ill and then died. Ill health was to hamper Nettleton's work the rest of his life and brought an end to his untiring, full-time work. Adding increased aggravation to the situation was the rise of a new evangelist in the Second Great Awakening: Charles Grandison

Finney. Converted in 1821, Finney had within three years launched his own evangelistic career, one that appeared to rival even George White-field in its extent and results—and to overshadow Nettleton's.

There are very human explanations for Nettleton's opposition to Finney: a natural resentment at being displaced as the revival's leading evangelist and the strain that his illness placed on his temper. Nettleton, however, based his opposition on Finney's sensational methods. Having always stressed a spirit of reverence in his services, Nettleton was put off by the irreverent prayers in Finney's meetings, what the older evan-gelist called "this talking to God as a man talks to his neighbor . . . telling the Lord a long story about A or B, and apparently with no other intent than to produce a kind of stage effect upon the individual in question, or upon the audience generally." A man such as Nettleton who was concerned with stressing restraint in the pulpit could hardly abide a preacher such as Finney, who sometimes descended to such depths in his sermons as "Why, sinner, I tell you, if you could climb to heaven, you would hurl God from his throne! Yes, hurl God from his throne! Oh, yes, if you could but get there, you would cut God's throat! Yes, you would cut God's throat!"

Finney responded pragmatically to his critics: "Show me a more excellent way. Show me the fruits of your ministry. . . . But do you expect me to abandon my own views and practices, and adopt yours . . . when the results justify my methods?" Nettleton replied, "It is said that God has blessed these measures to the conversion of sinners. . . . I answer: It is an acknowledged fact, that profane swearing, opposition to revivals, mock confessions, have all been overruled to the conviction and conversion of sinners. And shall we not encourage and defend these things?" Nettleton stressed that his concern was to save revivals from disrepute: "These evils, sooner or later, must be corrected. Somebody must speak, or silence will prove our ruin. Fire is an excellent thing in its place, and I am not afraid to see it blaze among briers and thorns; but when I see it kindling where it will ruin fences, and gardens, and houses, and burn up my friends, I cannot be silent."

In 1827 Nettleton, Finney, and several other preachers met in New Lebanon, New York, to discuss the conflict, but nothing was settled. Nettleton could not stop Finney or even alter the younger man's views and practices, as he would have preferred to do. To most churches, Finney appeared young, dynamic, energetic—and successful. Nettleton, prematurely aged by his illnesses and unable to preach as extensively as before, seemed to be a relic of a previous age. Still honored by those who respected his approach to revivals, Nettleton spent his last years preaching when his strength permitted and lecturing on evangelism to students in a new seminary in Connecticut that he had helped found. He died in 1844 of complications from gallstone surgery.

Asahel Nettleton and the Eastern Revivals

If Charles Finney is better remembered today than Nettleton, it may be in part because the public—even the Christian public—prefers the sensational to the sound. The record of converts from Nettleton's career—estimated at twenty-five thousand—is perhaps not as dramatic as the totals of some other evangelists. However, preachers who worked with Nettleton observed years later that there were relatively few "relapsed" converts after his meetings. In contrast, one writer quoted Finney himself as saying of his own converts that "the great body of them are a disgrace to religion." Only a year after Nettleton's death, Charles Finney, in a partial retraction, wrote, "The more I have seen of revivals, the more I am impressed with the importance of keeping excitement down. . . . I have learned to . . . feel much more confidence in apparent conversions that occur where there is greater calmness of mind." He had, in short, learned something of the evangelistic philosophy of Asahel Nettleton.

Suggestions for Further Reading

Keith J. Hardman. *Charles Grandison Finney, 1792-1875.* 1987. Reprint. Grand Rapids: Baker, 1990. [Hardman discusses in detail the conflict between Nettleton and Finney on pp. 104-49.]

John F. Thornbury. *God Sent Revival: The Story of Asahel Nettleton and the Second Great Awakening.* Welwyn, England: Evangelical Press, 1977. [Probably the most readable biography of Nettleton]

Bennet Tyler and Andrew A. Bonar. *Nettleton and His Labours.* 1854. Reprint. Edinburgh: Banner of Truth Trust, 1975. [A thorough biography by a close friend of Nettleton's (Tyler) but sometimes difficult reading]

"Brethren, We Have Met to Worship": The Frontier Camp Meetings

by Mark Sidwell

The revivals in the West differed dramatically from those in the East. In contrast to the earnest spirit of quiet devotion that marked revivals in the settled regions of the young nation, the frontier seemed to explode in revival. Although the noise and energy of the western revivals irritated some critics in the East, the results of the frontier awakenings confirmed, at least in part, their genuineness. The characteristic feature of the western revivals was the camp meeting, an institution that long outlived the awakening that spawned it. The story of the camp meeting's development and history is an essential part of the story of the Second Great Awakening in the West.

In 1800 fiery Presbyterian preacher James McGready called together one of the three tiny congregations he pastored in Logan County in southwestern Kentucky. Joining his flock for an outdoor communion service were four other preachers, three Presbyterians and a Methodist. What happened at the service surprised them all. Under the preaching of the gospel, people began to cry out in fear or even scream for God's mercy. After ten people were converted in this meeting, McGready quickly organized another for his second congregation, with the same results. By the time he had prepared an outdoor service for the third, news of the first two meetings had swelled the crowds. Hundreds of people attended the outdoor meeting, as ministers exhorted the crowds for several days. Both converted sinners and awakened saints streamed away when it was over. The camp meeting had been born.

Outdoor meetings were not new to Christianity, even on the American frontier. But the prolonged length of the meetings and especially the striking conversions marked the Logan County assemblies as something new and different. Their success inspired other preachers in the West to organize camp meetings. In 1801 a crowd estimated at between ten and twenty-five thousand people gathered at Cane Ridge, Kentucky (east of modern Lexington), for what was probably the largest camp meeting in history. Although Cane Ridge may have been the biggest, it was hardly the last, and it was typical of those that followed. Preachers addressed the crowds from hastily erected speaker's stands, from stumps, or even from the lower limbs of trees. Often several exhorters would thunder their messages to different parts of the crowd at the same time.

One characteristic of the Cane Ridge revival and other early camp meetings received widespread attention and criticism: the "exercises." Many people attending camp meetings displayed strange physical maladies as they came under conviction of sin. Barton Stone, leader of the Cane Ridge meeting, described several of these exercises:

> The falling exercise was very common among all classes. . . . The subject of this exercise would, generally, with a piercing scream, fall like a log on the floor, earth, or mud, and appear as dead. . . .
>
> The jerks cannot be so easily described. Sometimes the subject of the jerks would be affected in some one member of the body, and sometimes the whole system. When the head alone was affected, it would be jerked backward and forward, or from side to side, so quickly that the features of the face could not be distinguished. . . .
>
> The barking exercise (as opposers contemptuously called it,) was nothing but the jerks. A person affected with the jerks, especially in his head, would often make a grunt, or bark, if you please, from the suddenness of the jerk.

Actually, most of the exercises faded quickly after the initial blaze of the revival; only the falling exercise remained at all common long afterwards. How does the Christian explain these odd phenomena? Obviously mass hysteria and the uncultured nature of westerners played a part. Perhaps the best defense for "exercises" at camp meetings is offered by Bernard A. Weisberger in *They Gathered at the River*. In the East, he points out, conversion often came after a long period of soul-searching and contemplation. In the West, conversion often came more quickly. "When the traditionally slow cycle of guilt, despair, hope and assurance was compressed into a few days or hours," Weisberger notes, "its emotional states were agonizingly intensified." At any rate, those who focus on the unusual "side-effects" of the camp meetings miss the most important result: the changed lives of those touched by the revivals. Even secular historians acknowledge at least a temporary improvement in morals following the revivals.

There were different types of meetings. The sacramental meeting, where communion was taken, as in Logan County, was popular in the early days. Union meetings, where several denominations (usually Presbyterian, Baptist, and Methodist) joined, may have been larger. Folks would travel for miles to go to the meetings, bringing food, tents, and other supplies so that they could stay in the open for several days. Camp meetings were of course a major social event in isolated frontier life, but organizers tried to keep the spiritual purpose in the forefront. In addition to scheduling sermons and prayer meetings during the day, promoters urged upon the campers times of private devotion and meditation.

The sermons, though, were the heart of the meetings. Frontier preachers tried to speak to their audiences in terms that the common man could understand. It is difficult to capture on the printed page the rhythm and power of the camp meeting speakers without caricaturing the preachers somewhat. Consider the following example from an Alabama camp meeting:

> Breethring, I see yonder a man that's a sinner! I know he's a sinner! Thar he stands, a missuble old crittur, with his head a-blossomin' for the grave! A few more short years, and d-o-w-n he'll go to perdition, lessen the Lord have mer-cy on him! Come up here, you old hoary-headed sinner, a-n-d git down upon your knees, a-n-d put up your cry for the Lord to snatch you from the bottomless pit! You're ripe for the devil; you're b-o-u-n-d for hell, and the Lord knows what'll become you!

Despite whatever homiletic deficiencies existed, it cannot be denied that the listeners understood the message and responded.

Simon Kenton certainly understood it. Kenton was a famous frontier scout who served under George Rogers Clark during the American Revolution, General "Mad Anthony" Wayne in the Fallen Timbers campaign, and General William Henry Harrison in the War of 1812. He was a friend and companion of Daniel Boone during the exploration and settlement of Kentucky and had once carried the wounded Boone to safety during an Indian attack. In 1808 he was living in Ohio, where he was a general of the militia. In that year he attended a Methodist camp meeting under the Reverend Bennett Maxey. After listening to the preaching, Kenton took Maxey into the woods. Swearing the preacher to secrecy, the frontiersman confessed all the sins that troubled him, especially the killing he had done in battle. Could God forgive him? the hardy Kenton wondered with tears in his eyes. Maxey assured him of God's love and of His power to forgive. After praying with the minister, Kenton ran back to the meeting grounds. When the preacher arrived, he found the new convert telling everyone of the change. "General," said Maxey, "I thought we were to keep the matter a secret."

"Oh, it's too glorious for that," replied Kenton. "If I had all the world here, I would tell of the mercy and goodness of God!"

Despite such stories of triumph, camp meetings received their share of criticism. Some of it centered on the abuses. Eastern evangelist Asahel Nettleton, for example, found it difficult to separate the wheat of genuine revival from the chaff of the excesses. He wrote,

> My impression is, that the most enlightened and sincere friends of vital piety, who had the best opportunity of being intimately acquainted with the revivals . . . believe them to have been a real work of the Holy Spirit; or, at least, to have been productive of a number of genuine conversions. But that this work of grace was attended, and finally overshadowed, disgraced, and terminated, by fanaticism and disorders of the most distressing character, will not, probably, now be questioned by any competent judges.

Others were worried by the doctrinal defections of a few of the leaders. Barton Stone, for example, the leader of the Cane Ridge meeting, began proclaiming views that seemed to call the doctrine of the Trinity into question. Later Stone broke with the Presbyterians and became one of the founders of the Disciples of Christ, who taught the necessity of baptism by immersion for salvation. A handful of revival leaders even joined the Shakers, a frontier sect which thought that its founder, Mother Ann Lee, was the female incarnation of God and that all sexual relations were sinful. Most leaders of the camp meetings, however, remained doctrinally orthodox.

As the years passed, the camp meeting became more exclusively a Methodist institution. Presbyterians—put off by the irregularities, the uneducated ministry, and the doctrinal deviations of men such as Barton Stone—withdrew from the camp meetings. Baptists—uneasy working with "competing" denominations and preferring more distinctly church-oriented evangelistic activities—also withdrew. Bishop Francis Asbury illustrated this fact when he said, "The Methodists are all for camp-meetings; the Baptists are for public baptizings."

The Methodists, after they came to dominate camp meetings, brought a sense of order and organization. They made the meetings annual events, built established camp grounds, and formed camp meeting associations. The meetings definitely became more orderly under Methodist discipline, but there seems to have been little diminution of spiritual power. After noting the absence of the "bodily agitations" at an 1820 Tennessee camp meeting, a camp meeting leader added, "The work of conviction in the hearts of the sinners has been regular, powerful, and deep . . . their rejoicing scriptural and rational."

By the beginning of the Civil War, camp meetings had passed their peak. Even so, the institution did not die. Methodist camp meeting grounds actually became more permanent, with auditoriums replacing open clearings and sturdy cabins replacing tents. When the Holiness movement arose late in the nineteenth century with its announced aim of calling Methodism back to the devout life advocated by John Wesley, it too utilized camp meetings to promote its teachings and edify its followers. Even today some smaller Holiness and Methodist groups still hold annual camp meetings.

The heritage of the camp meetings is a rich one. As is often the case with revivals, it is virtually impossible to measure the most important result: the number of souls saved and saints edified by those meetings. Still, some of the flavor of the camp meetings is found in the many hymns that originally lofted from those forest clearings, songs such as "On Jordan's Stormy Banks" and "Beulah Land." George Atkins embodied much of the camp meeting spirit in one of his songs:

> *Brethren, we have met to worship and adore the Lord our God;*
> *Will you pray with all your power, while we try to preach the Word?*
> *All is vain unless the Spirit of the Holy One comes down;*
> *Brethren, pray, and holy manna will be showered all around.*

Suggestions for Further Reading

Charles A. Johnson. *The Frontier Camp Meeting.* Dallas: Southern Methodist University Press, 1955. [Probably the best overall history of camp meetings but weighted toward the period of Methodist dominance]

Keith J. Hardman. *The Spiritual Awakeners.* Chicago: Moody Press, 1983. [See pp. 129-46.]

"Has He a Horse?":
The Saga of the Circuit Riders

by Richard Rupp and Mark Minnick

Settlers on the frontier had a saying to describe stormy weather: "There is nothing out today but crows and Methodist preachers." Certainly few preachers of the gospel have shown the courage and perseverance of the Methodist circuit riders. They were agents of the Great Awakening in the West, the establishers of Methodism in this country, and most important, the messengers of the saving gospel of Jesus Christ to thousands of lost souls.

"Rooted and grounded in love, settled and established in sound doctrine; but in everything else he should be as movable as a soldier on the land or a sailor on the sea." Such was the philosophy that motivated a group of America's hardiest frontiersmen, the circuit-riding preachers. It is to the dogged persistence of the circuit riders that Christians owe much for the intrinsically religious fiber our nation retains today.

Souls with Heavenly Fire

Circuit riding took its precedent from the fluid examples of Britishers John Wesley and George Whitefield, both of whom carried their ministries from city to city. Wesley said, "The world is my parish," and the early Methodist itinerants showed every evidence of having captured his spirit. It was largely the Methodist denomination that made use of frontier circuit riders. The Presbyterian, Baptist, and Congregational groups were characterized by ponderous progress, a peculiarity which added much to the religious prominence Methodism enjoyed in nineteenth-century America. One historian records that in 1784 the Methodists had fewer than 15,000 members, 43 circuits, and 83 itinerants. By 1844 the denomination had 1,069,000 members, almost 4,000 circuit riders, and more than 7,000 local preachers. Such a phenomenal growth in only sixty years was largely the result of Methodism's practical structure. With the founding of a new settlement, an ordinary layman would often take the initiative in inviting his neighbors to his cabin for religious services. A religious

Faith of Our Fathers: Scenes from American Church History

"society" would be formed and brought under the "wing" of a circuit rider who answered to a conference bishop, the church official responsible for supplying several circuits with preachers.

The arrangement was flexible; yet it was this advantage that contributed heavily to the strain endured by itinerants. There simply were not enough preachers to man the circuits. Often a rider would have more than two dozen preaching stations and spend as long as a month making a single round. It is no wonder that Dr. Abel Stevens, a leading Methodist historian, states: "Nearly half of those [circuit riders] whose deaths are recorded [by the end of the eighteenth century] died before they were thirty years old; about two thirds died before they had spent 12 years in the laborious service." Had these preachers been looking for an easy ministry they certainly would have avoided the circuits.

One of the worst hardships of the itinerancy was the days of endless travel. The book of Methodist regulations, *The Discipline,* had as a "rule of thumb" that the preachers rise at four in the morning to allow time for travel. We might think that in the desolate frontier a man might easily avoid such a technicality and "sleep in" on occasion, but even had a rider wished to bend such a rule the sheer bulk of miles between preaching stations ruled out all possibility of indulging himself. And it was not only the distance they traveled that strained the circuit riders. The terrain itself was a rugged factor to be reckoned with daily. A pioneer preacher in Louisiana wrote, "Every day I travel I have to swim through creeks or swamps, and I am wet from head to feet, and some days from morning to night I am dripping with water. My horse's legs are now skinned and rough to his hock joints, and I have rheumatism in all my joints . . . what I have suffered in body and mind my pen is not able to communicate to you." This would be a bleak commentary had the preacher ended here, but hastening on he records, "But this I can say, while my body is wet with water and chilled with cold my soul is filled with heavenly fire, and I can say with St. Paul, 'But none of these things shall move me, neither count I my life dear unto myself, so that I might finish my course with joy.' " This was the spirit that conquered America. That a circuit rider was in continual peril on the lonely trails was a matter of course. That he might be weary, burn with fever, or shake with the ague was insignificant. Everything, including his very life, must be subservient to the grand task of carrying the message of God's Word.

An Air of Establishment

The circuit-riding preachers were in one sense the first to truly tame the wilderness. To be sure, rugged souls ventured to build cabins and clear paths through the forests, but the settlements never really lost their wildness until the pioneers had a preacher. The desolate wilderness could penetrate even the hardiest of pioneer spirits with discouragement and despair, benumbing entire settlements. But with the arrival of the circuit rider came an air of secure establishment that bred confidence in the most forlorn surroundings.

The itinerant preachers themselves sensed the great influence they held in fostering the moral constitution of America, and had it not been for this sense of responsibility, they surely would have deserted their posts. It certainly was not material prosperity that kept them in the saddle. In principle the Methodists paid their preachers, but the discrepancy between principle and practice was sometimes tragedy. There are accounts of preachers selling their boots to feed their families or parting with precious wool topcoats to pay for the shoeing of a lame horse. Henry Bascom, a well-known West Virginian itinerant, traveled more than three thousand miles and preached to more than four hundred congregations during one particular year. For that service he received twelve dollars and ten cents. In addition to sheer poverty, the circuit riders were often placed in the worst accommodation; and yet no matter how crowded, smelly, filthy, or insect-and-disease-ridden the cabins, he was bound by the very nature of his calling to accept his lodgings without complaint.

Such sacrifice was not entirely unrewarded, and the names of such itinerants as Bascom, James Axley, Francis Asbury, Jacob Young, and Peter Cartwright became almost household words for the pioneers. At times their recognition extended even to the political leaders of the day. Cartwright tells an amusing story about Axley and himself as guests of Governor and Mrs. Edward Tiffin of Ohio. During the meal Axley acquired a number of bones on the side of his plate. Seeing a dog in another room, the well-meaning frontiersman whistled for it and threw the bones on the floor next to the table. The amused governor had difficulty repressing his laughter. Later, when Cartwright told Axley that he had committed an error in etiquette, Axley was chagrined. No one had better intentions than this rough-and-ready preacher who had been looking forward to sleeping for the first time in a plastered house.

Perhaps the greatest reward, though, was seeing churches spring up all across the land. Jess Walker, a circuit rider of the early nineteenth century, entered St. Louis in 1818 with the words, "I have come in the name of Christ to take Saint Louis, and by the grace of God I will do it." God was with him in his efforts, for within a year he had a church of sixty members and a free school for poor children. It was this same man who introduced Methodism to a tiny settlement perched precariously on the south shore of Lake Michigan in 1830; the cluster of cabins later became known by a universally recognized name—Chicago.

Faith of Our Fathers: Scenes from American Church History

Asbury's Wide Circuit

A better insight into the life of an itinerant can be produced through a glance at possibly the best known of all circuit riders—Francis Asbury. For more than forty years this man of God braved the elements day and night that he might turn the whole of America into one great circuit.

Appointed by Wesley in 1771 to fill the position of "general assistant" for the work of Methodism in America, Asbury was twenty-six when he entered the itinerancy. From that point, the name of Francis Asbury dominated the American religious scene until his death in 1816. Wherever he went new churches were formed, new circuits laid out, and hosts of preachers raised to carry the gospel to remote villages. He is described as roving everywhere. If a poor itinerant was in trouble with local officials, Asbury was ready with personal influence to protect him or with his purse to pay any fine. If there was a man posted in an almost inaccessible region and in want of fellowship, Asbury's path was sure to cross his so that the lonely preacher might be encouraged. And wherever a little band of adventurers planted themselves in the forest they were sure to soon be taken into Asbury's ever-extending circuit.

Asbury, like most circuit riders, was without the benefit of higher education, but his devotion to the Word and exercises in prayer were almost without parallel. Having no place to study but the saddle, he nevertheless gained a superior knowledge of both the Greek and Hebrew testaments, and it is said that he was the intellectual peer of almost any man he met.

In prayer Asbury especially distinguished himself. There are records in his *Journal* of set seasons for this devotion. During one period he prayed for at least three hours every day. Later he spent ten minutes of every waking hour praying and wrote, "My desire is that prayer should mix with every thought, with every wish, with every word, and with every action, that all might ascend as a holy, acceptable sacrifice to God."

At one point in his ministry, Asbury was driven by sheer necessity to seek a short rest near the White Sulphur Springs (now in West Virginia). A friend recorded that during that vacation Asbury "[reads] about one hundred pages a day; usually prays in public five times a day; preaches in the open air every other day; and lectures in prayer-meeting every evening." Such a schedule for regular pastoral duties is enough to bring consternation to most preachers, but as a vacation the thought is intolerable!

Wives of Rarest Caliber

Asbury often recommended that his circuit riders give themselves to celibacy, for the most taxed area of an itinerant's life was his family. The meager income of most circuit riders made it impossible for them to maintain families without "locating" when they married. The majority took Asbury's advice and gave themselves to lives of solitude, but for those who ventured to raise a family the hardships of the ministry were compounded considerably. Though he might reside in a given community, the preacher was still responsible for a broad area, and even his residence had to be periodically uprooted due to the two-year maximum any preacher was allowed to spend on a given circuit.

Perhaps it was the wife of such a man, though, who had the hardest lot. Stretching pennies until they covered days and struggling to maintain the barest semblance of a home amid constant activity called for a woman of the rarest caliber. The preacher himself could always fall back on the exaltation of the preaching to fill his soul and compensate for the loss of worldly goods and natural comforts, but for his wife the loss of all security spelled an extreme test of dedication and faith to meet each unpromising day with a thankful heart. Hers was the task of serving while rarely seeing the results of her husband's ministry for which she sacrificed so much.

Methodists Everywhere

Despite the hardships of the ministry, circuit riding seemed to attract the strongest young men, and by the time of Asbury's death he had seen hundreds join the ranks. The circuits were large, and the 1800s brought a tremendous surge in population; yet somehow the Methodist itinerants appeared everywhere. An amusing example of this is recorded from the life of a rugged preacher by the name of Nolley, who was in a remote section of Mississippi when he noticed some wagon tracks that appeared to be quite recent. No circuit rider worth his salt ever ignored the possibility to make a new contact; so Nolley followed the wagon tracks until they ended in a fresh clearing. A settler had just a few moments before begun to unload his wagon. Nolley introduced himself to the new family, but when the settler found out who the visitor was he expressed the greatest disgust, exclaiming, "Another Methodist preacher! I left Virginia for Georgia to get clear of them. There they got my wife and daughter. So I come here, and here is one before I can get my wagon unloaded!" "My friend," said Nolley, "if you go to Heaven you'll find Methodist preachers there; if you go to Hell, I'm afraid you'll find some there; and you see how it is on earth, so you had better make terms with us and be at peace." The "before I can get my wagon unloaded" incident became a standard joke at later conference meetings. There's humor in the incident, but it also indicates the splendid determination and spirit that played major roles in taming this country.

Faith of Our Fathers: Scenes from American Church History

The Rider's Vision

In Washington, D.C., stands the statue of a worn rider astride a weary horse. The horseman is a bronze likeness of Francis Asbury, a tribute to him and all the hundreds of young circuit riders who traced the trails of early America. Faithfully rendered by the artist with every detail of extreme exhaustion, the statue bears one attribute that escapes all but the keenest scrutiny. Out from under the brim of the low hat peer eyes alive with spiritual strength—eyes so true to the character of circuit-riding preachers, for the eyes reflect a sense of a great calling, dreams for a mighty nation, and the indication of purpose to call a great country to devotion to God.

"Has he a horse?" was the query of the old Methodist bishops when considering a new candidate. No preacher-carrying horses use the roads of America today, but God have mercy on this land if she lacks men with the vision of those who rode their horses so well.

Suggestions for Further Reading

Peter Cartwright. *Autobiography of Peter Cartwright.* 1856. Reprint. Nashville: Abingdon, 1984.

Keith J. Hardman. "Apostles on Horseback: Francis Asbury and the Methodist Circuit Riders." *Christian History,* vol. 8, no. 3 (1989), pp. 22-23.

————. *The Spiritual Awakeners.* Chicago: Moody Press, 1983. [See pp. 93-108.]

Charles A. Johnson. *The Frontier Camp Meeting.* Dallas: Southern Methodist University Press, 1955. [Chapter 8 (pp. 145-69) deals specifically with the circuit riders.]

L. C. Rudolph. *Francis Asbury.* 1966. Reprint. Nashville: Abingdon, 1983.

Sowing on Burma's Plain: The Story of Adoniram Judson

by Christa G. Habegger and Gene Elliott

By spurring America's first great foreign missions movement, the Second Great Awakening touched not only the United States but also nations across the seas. Perhaps the greatest, and certainly the most famous, of the early heroes of American foreign missions was Adoniram Judson, missionary to Burma. His story is one of pain, hardship, sorrow, and suffering but also one of faith, courage, and dedication.

On a cold autumn night in 1808, young Adoniram Judson stopped at a Connecticut country inn, his mind weighed down with a spiritual challenge he had just received from a young preacher. Asking for a room, Judson was told that there was but one available—one next to the room of a dying man. With an air of self-assurance, he told the innkeeper that death meant nothing to him and that he would take the room.

Judson tried to sleep, but the sounds next door—the muffled groans of the dying man, the boards creaking under the weight of his attendants—kept him awake. The next morning he inquired about the sick man to the innkeeper. "He is dead," said the landlord. "Do you know who he was?" asked the young man. Yes, the keeper answered, a young student from Brown University named Jacob Eames.

Judson paled. The dead man was none other than a close college friend, a self-professed intellectual, Deist, and wit with whom Judson had spent many hours talking, laughing, and planning the future. Judson could not even continue his journey until late in the day; he remembered years later that as he thought of Eames, words echoed in his ears— "Dead! lost! lost!" Grieved, he returned home and later went to Andover Seminary, hoping to find some comfort for his soul in studying for the ministry. On December 2, 1808, Adoniram Judson gave his heart to Jesus Christ and found peace.

After his conversion, Judson became burdened with the need of the Far East for missionaries. He joined forces with a group of young, zealous seminary students to help found a Congregationalist mission board, the American Board of Commissioners for Foreign Missions (ABCFM). Judson and another one of the students, Luther Rice, eventually sailed to the Far East under the ABCFM. Ironically, Rice and Judson changed their theological views before commencing their work and became Baptists. Rice returned to the United States to raise support among American Baptists while Judson stayed in Asia. Just as the conflict between Paul and Barnabas providentially resulted in the creation of two missionary efforts in New Testament days (Acts 15:36-41), so the action of Judson and Rice drew the Baptists to join the Congregationalists in sending missionaries to the field.

In 1810, before going to the foreign field, Judson had met Ann Hasseltine of Bradford, Massachusetts, and fell in love. Two years later they were married. Judson knew when he asked for Ann's hand that his request would involve great sacrifice: Ann would probably never see her family again. The young missionaries intended to live and die in Asia. They set sail shortly after their wedding.

They went to Burma, an Asian nation adjacent to British-occupied India. The couple applied themselves immediately to the tasks of setting up housekeeping in Rangoon and learning the Burmese customs and language. Burma was not known as a nation friendly to foreigners, especially religious ones. The empire was governed by a despot whose whims were law. He and others before him had made it clear that the religion of the land was Buddhism and that renouncing it was a capital offense.

Language study demanded as much as twelve hours a day of the Judsons. Adoniram had hired a Burmese scholar to teach him the language so that he could translate the Bible and other material into Burmese. Ann, by working closely with native women in day-to-day housekeeping, was actually able to communicate far more quickly and easily than her studious husband. Thus, she was of incalculable aid to him both in their dealings with the natives and in the work of translation.

Their efforts to win souls were not rewarded immediately. People with whom they were able to make friends said, ''Our religion is good for us, yours for you.'' One unusual friendship the Judsons made was with a Burmese viceroy newly appointed by the king to work in Rangoon. He invited the Judsons to the government house often. Besides providing companionship, this friendship afforded the Judsons a degree of protection from harassment.

In September 1815 Ann gave birth to a son. The baby was a great novelty in the community and a precious addition to the missionary household. But his life was tragically short. At eight months little Roger died of a fever. Despite their anguish at his death, the Judsons' faith remained strong. One day, shortly after the baby's death, the viceroy's wife announced that she had arranged a procession of elephants in memory of the child. She hoped it would help to distract the couple from their loss. Together she and the Judsons were led into the jungle on the huge beasts by a guard of thirty men. There they dismounted and reclined upon mats while the vicereine made garlands of blossoms for the Judsons and served them fruit.

Even though the mission house was frequently filled with Burmese who were curious about the "teachers' " religion, it was not until 1817 that Judson could write home that anyone had seriously inquired about the gospel. This first sincere inquirer was a respected native scholar who came after having read two of Judson's printed tracts. Barely were introductions made when the scholar astonished the missionary by asking, "How long a time will it take me to learn the religion of Jesus?" After a short stay the scholar returned to his home, unconverted but determined to consider the matter of "Judson's religion."

During these first years of their missionary work, the Judsons were frequently ill from fevers and various sicknesses to which foreigners in the East were susceptible, and they were forced to endure painful separations more than once while one of them took a therapeutic sea voyage to recover health. Yet their letters to friends in America and to each other reveal that their primary concern was not for their health or comfort but rather for their ministry to needy Burmese. Ann wrote on several occasions that she did not mind what happened to her as long as the work of the gospel were furthered. But was it indeed being furthered? They must have wondered. In 1819, six years after their arrival in Burma, they still did not have a single convert.

In April of that year, Judson decided to risk persecution by building his own *zavat,* a place of worship. It was a courageous move, but it took perhaps even greater courage for native Burmese to meet with them in the new structure. The congregation began to grow, however, and in May the first Burmese convert made a profession of faith. In the years to come, many others were converted, among them the native scholar who had been the first to express an interest in the missionaries' teachings.

The missionaries grew alarmed because of the opposition their converts were facing. In December of 1819 Judson and another missionary who had joined the couple at Rangoon traveled to Ava, the capital, where they hoped to gain the king's official permission to continue their teaching. They took with them a petition and a richly covered Bible to give to the Golden Presence, as the Burmese called their king. They returned to Rangoon unsuccessful. The king had been interested in American dress and customs and impressed by Judson's knowledge of the Burmese tongue, but upon hearing that "the teachers" professed belief in "one eternal God, and that beside Him, there is no God," he sent them away, having refused both their gift and their petition. In Rangoon the missionaries feared that when the converts learned that the king had refused to extend protection to them, they would falter in their faith. Instead the new Christians responded with renewed boldness.

In 1821, after having already traveled once to Calcutta for treatment of a liver ailment, Ann was again forced to undertake a journey—this time back to the United States—if she were going to survive at all. It was a difficult separation, but the trip proved in one way to be a blessing in disguise. On her way back, in England and Scotland, and later in the United States, she gathered prayer support among Christians for their labors and heightened interest in their mission work.

During the two years his wife was away, Adoniram Judson again visited Ava along with a medical missionary whom the Golden Presence wished to consult. The two men had numerous audiences with the king, who not only inquired about the doctor's medical knowledge but also seemed eager to learn more about the mission work. He was surprised to learn that some Burmese had actually embraced Judson's religion. On hearing that Judson preached in Burmese every Sunday in his own *zavat,* the king said unexpectedly, "Let's hear how you preach." Judson then had an unprecedented opportunity to present the gospel in Burma's pagan court.

The king wished the men to stay in Ava indefinitely. The doctor remained in the city while Judson returned to Rangoon to await his wife's return. Soon after her arrival, the couple committed their work in Rangoon to capable native Christians and made their plans to move to Ava. There they lost no time in setting up another *zavat,* and Ann started a school for little girls.

War broke out between Burma and Great Britain in 1824, and suddenly foreigners were objects of hatred and suspicion. The missionaries, despite their close ties with many officials in the city, were not exempt from persecution. One evening in June when the Judsons were finishing their supper, a dozen Burmese rushed into their house and arrested Adoniram. Binding him tightly, they dragged him to the "death prison," a filthy place from which few prisoners were released alive. Ann set about immediately to secure her husband's release. While Adoniram was subjected to conditions reminiscent of the Spanish Inquisition, Ann applied to influential friends for assistance, but to no avail. The governor of the city, who sympathized with Ann, was unable to have Adoniram freed, but he did make it possible for Ann to visit the prison daily with food for her husband.

During this bleak period of their lives, Ann gave birth to a tiny daughter, Maria. The child was undernourished, Ann being weakened by continual strain on her physical and emotional resources. When Adoniram was moved to a town several miles away, Ann followed and continued her efforts to secure his release. While there, she nearly died of a violent fever. During her illness, there was no one to care for little

Maria. Judson managed to get permission to leave the prison once a day to beg milk of native mothers for the starving child until a Burmese nurse offered to care for her.

Meanwhile the war was all but won by the British. When it looked as though the white prisoners would be released any day by the victorious army, Judson was transferred back to the foul prison at Ava where his services were demanded as an interpreter for the Burmese. Judson, though half-dead from fever and maltreatment, helped with the negotiations with the British. Part of the resulting treaty demanded that the Burmese turn over Adoniram, as well as Ann and Maria. On hearing that the Judsons were to be released to the British, the king retorted, "They are my people, and shall not go." The Judsons were not fooled by his protective manner; they suspected that he was reluctant to lose Judson's valuable skills in negotiating with the British.

On March 6, 1826, Adoniram was finally released by the Burmese. The Judson family, thin and worn from the hardships they had endured, returned to Rangoon. Ann wrote soon after their arrival: "We now consider our future missionary prospects as bright, indeed; and our only anxiety is to be once more in that situation where our time will be exclusively devoted to the instruction of the heathen."

Judson, sharing Ann's optimism and finding the converts prospering in Rangoon, felt that it was time for them to begin a mission work elsewhere. He took Ann and the baby to Amherst, the new capital of provinces under British control. Convinced that both mother and child were comfortably settled there and were recovering their strength, Adoniram agreed to travel again for the British in further treaty negotiations. But in his absence, Ann died of a fever, and within a few months, little Maria followed.

Judson, having buried both wife and daughter beneath the same hopia tree, was a broken man. He withdrew from other people and began to purge his life of many things that he held dear. He gave up the reading of literature and destroyed his personal papers, which he feared would call undue attention to himself. He gave his Burmese property to the mission board and fasted and prayed for forty days.

Judson emerged from this trial with an intensified desire to serve God. He expanded his work, and in 1834 he married Sarah Boardman, the widow of another American missionary. With a happy, stable home life helping support him, Adoniram was able to finish his translation of the Bible into Burmese. Sarah proved a wonderful help in translation work herself. She translated part one of *Pilgrim's Progress* into Burmese as well as numerous tracts and Bible lessons. In 1845, however, Sarah also fell ill. Forced to return to the United States, the Judsons got only as far as the island of St. Helena in the South Atlantic, where Sarah died. Shortly before her death, she penned a poem to encourage her husband. One stanza read,

Then gird thine armor on, love,
Nor faint thou by the way,
Till Buddha shall fall, and Burmah's sons
Shall own Messiah's sway.

Thirty-two years after leaving America for the East, Adoniram Judson returned to Boston with his motherless children. He was surprised and a little embarrassed by the adulation he received from American Christians. To share the results of the ministry in Burma, Judson asked a female Christian writer, twenty-nine-year-old Emily Chubbuck, to help him write a biography of Sarah. The work became literally a labor of love as the old missionary and the young writer fell in love, married, and headed for Rangoon, the city of Adoniram's first ministry in Burma.

Judson's final ministry in Burma was comparatively short. After finishing his Burmese-English dictionary in 1849, Adoniram fell ill. He took a sea voyage early in 1850 in hopes of shaking the sickness. Instead he weakened and slipped out of life on April 12, 1850. Besides a wife and family, he left behind over sixty churches, more than one hundred and fifty missionaries, and at least seven thousand converts. On the cover of a book he used in his research for the Burmese dictionary, Adoniram Judson penciled his own appropriate epitaph:

In joy or sorrow, health or pain,
Our course is upward still.
We sow on Burmah's plain,
We reap on Zion's hill.

Suggestions for Further Reading

Courtney Anderson. *To the Golden Shore: The Life of Adoniram Judson.* 1956. Reprint. Valley Forge, Pa.: Judson Press, 1987.
Ruth A. Tucker. *From Jerusalem to Irian Jaya: A Biographical History of Christian Missions.* Grand Rapids: Zondervan, 1983. [See pp. 121-31.]

John Chavis

by Rachel C. Larson

Often ignored in church history are the preachers of the gospel who reached out to the lower classes, people such as the rescue mission workers who extended compassion to the "down-and-out." Likewise, orthodox black ministers have received short shrift from many liberal historians. Yet the Second Great Awakening in particular saw the emergence of devout black preachers of the gospel who carried a burden for the salvation not only of their own people but for others as well. One was former slave Richard Allen, who founded the African Methodist Episcopal Church, one of the largest black denominations in the United States. Another was the subject of this article, black Presbyterian John Chavis.

John Chavis, described as "a full-blooded negro of dark brown complexion," was born to free black parents in Granville County, North Carolina, about 1763, close to the time the French and Indian War ended. He entered his teen-age years during the American Revolutionary War and was one of five thousand freed blacks who volunteered to fight for the Patriot cause even though not required to do so.

According to tradition, Chavis was the first black to study at Princeton. Though faculty records prior to 1781 are fragmentary and Chavis's name does not appear on a graduation roster, his name does appear on a list of nongraduating attenders. There are two stories of how John Chavis got to Princeton. The first was that he was sent to college by two Southerners to settle a bet they had made whether a Negro could learn Latin and Greek. If this tale is true, whoever gambled against Chavis lost, for the young black became a good Latin scholar and a fair Greek student. Chavis learned both languages well enough to teach them to his own students in later years and to use them as tools for his sermon preparation. The second explanation for Chavis's enrollment is based on the fact that Presbyterians believed in a well-educated clergy. Some influential North Carolina Presbyterians who heard of John's desire to preach and who were impressed with that desire and with his abilities arranged for him to go to their college.

Faith of Our Fathers: Scenes from American Church History

In September of 1780 a church synod committee meeting at Princeton received a request from the Hanover, Virginia, presbytery "praying that some missionaries be sent . . . to preach the gospel . . . to form people into regular congregations . . . and to undertake the education of their youth." Chavis went to Virginia from Princeton with the Reverend Samuel Davies and worked with him in the Hanover and Lexington presbyteries. Chavis also continued his education, studying under William Graham, also a Princeton graduate, at Liberty Hall Academy (today's Washington and Lee University).

In October 1799 Chavis applied to the Lexington, Virginia, presbytery for a preaching license. He was described in the minutes of the presbytery meeting as a man "of unquestionably good fame." For his upcoming trials, John was assigned to prepare an exegesis in Latin on the theme *in quo consistat salvatio ab peccato* ("in whom [or which] salvation from sin consists"). He was then assigned to preach a sermon on Acts 16:31—"Believe on the Lord Jesus Christ, and thou shalt be saved." Chavis testified of his salvation, was tried, questioned, and then licensed that same day. He began his licensed preaching career as a supply preacher. The following summer he requested a transfer to the Hanover, Virginia, presbytery.

Meanwhile the church general assembly hired Chavis "as a missionary among people of his own colour." The 1802 proceedings relate that John had "executed his mission with great diligence, fidelity, and prudence." Chavis undertook various evangelistic tours through southern Virginia and northern North Carolina. George Wortham, the son of one of Chavis's pupils, described Chavis's preaching: "His English was remarkably pure. . . . His explanations clear and concise, and his views . . . entirely orthodox. . . . His sermons abound in strong, common sense views and happy illustrations without any effort at oratory or sensational appeal to the passion of his hearers. He had certainly read God's Word much and meditated deeply on it."

On one preaching tour Chavis preached sixty-eight messages, delivered eight exhortations, preached to several religious and missionary societies, and administered the Lord's Supper. The collection given him on that tour totaled $1.86. Never discouraged, Chavis thanked the Lord for using him to save souls and for providing him with food and lodging.

Attendance figures recorded for services reveal that Chavis preached to integrated audiences, with blacks constituting between twelve and twenty-five per cent of his audiences. Chavis was grieved that many of the slaves preferred the more emotional and less literary exhortations of their fellow slaves to his well-prepared Bible expositions.

Throughout Chavis's life he faced the special stress of being a free black. His education and income allowed him a lifestyle more like that of whites than of slaves; yet he felt a consistent loyalty to his own race and was burdened to win them and teach them Scriptural truths. Pre–Civil War laws barred blacks from full acceptance in white society; at the same time free blacks were not really trusted by fellow blacks.

The years of Chavis's evangelistic work coincided with the sweeping of the Second Great Awakening into the South Atlantic states. Some were so elated by the effects of the revival that they referred to the movement as "the beginning of the millennium." Ann Smith of Granville, North Carolina, wrote to her relatives in South Carolina of the "meetings where this great work was going" forward under Chavis.

By 1809 Chavis concentrated his work in northern North Carolina. Although he continued to preach over the next twenty years in Granville, Orange, and Wake counties, his primary occupation became his school in Raleigh, North Carolina. It is probably as an educator that he won his greatest acclaim. Historian Philip Foner says, "It was John Chavis who was undoubtedly one of the most famous teachers, white or black, in early America." Chavis ran preparatory schools in North Carolina from 1808 to 1830. He taught Greek, Latin, English, math, and rhetoric to both boys and girls, some of whom were from the state's more prominent families.

When Chavis founded his school it was his intention to instruct blacks and whites together. Opposition led to a change, however, and the *Raleigh Register* on August 25, 1808, advertised "a white school in the day time" and "an Evening School for the purpose of instructing children of Colour."

Though many slave states showed little interest in and sometimes even prohibited the education of blacks, North Carolina did not place restrictions on its education until 1838. Over forty per cent of North Carolina's free Negro adults were listed as literate in 1850. The largest number of literate blacks—slave and free—were in Wake County where Chavis had his school.

Reflecting his own Biblical training at Princeton, Chavis believed that education should build character. "Those who think proper to put their children under my care may rely upon the strictest attention being paid not only to their education but to their morals which I determine an important part of their Education."

Chavis was well respected as an educator. Joseph Gales, editor of the *Raleigh Register,* attended an examination at Chavis's school, then published the following editorial on April 19, 1830:

> To witness a well regulated school, composed to this class of persons—to see them setting an example in both behaviour and scholarship which their white superiors might take pride in imitating, was a cheering spectacle to the philanthropist. . . . The object of the respectable teacher was to impress on the scholars,

> the fact, that though they occupied an inferior and subordinate status in society and were possessed of but limited privileges, . . . they might become useful in their particular sphere, by making a proper improvement of the advantages offered them.

But just at the time Chavis's work began to attract notice, Nat Turner, a self-styled black slave preacher, led a rebellion in Southampton, Virginia. Already suspicious that the church might breed insurrection by offering independence to blacks, and with Turner's action confirming the state's worst fears, North Carolina passed a law in 1831 making it unlawful for freed blacks to preach or teach in any meeting "where slaves of different families are collected together." The presbytery urged white ministers and licensed preachers to preach at least one sermon each Sunday to blacks and to seek laymen to watch over their spiritual interests. Then the presbytery had a collection taken for John Chavis. It totaled $52.42.

But Chavis did not expect charity. He launched a career as a publisher of exegetical sermons, selling his sermons for 15¢ a copy. He also continued to teach free black children, because the law did not say it was illegal to teach free blacks, but he was criticized even for this. In 1837 the presbytery offered a token solution to the financial part of Chavis's problem by voting to retire Chavis, paying him $50 annually for the rest of his life. Chavis, who had already carried on correspondence with some of his former students, now exhausted himself through extensive letter writing, believing that if he could not teach or preach legally through the spoken word, he could at least use his pen.

Despite the personal hurt inflicted on Chavis and his ministry, Chavis's own view of slavery never varied. The social views of most free blacks in the South tended to be conservative, for the emancipation of slaves would have robbed them of their special status and increased competition for jobs. Although Chavis believed "slavery is a gross national evil," he was "clearly of the opinion that immediate emancipation would be to entail the greatest earthly curse upon my brethren." He also knew that his views might be unpopular among some blacks and among abolitionists. "I suppose," he wrote in a letter to a former student, "if they knew how I said, they would take my life." He did not believe that "the hands of either a Democrat or a Republican Government are sufficient to restrain the corruption of human nature." Only God's hand could restrain that. Chavis predicted the Civil War, saying, "The volcano will burst and the lava will spread far and wide to destructive ruin."

Some blacks of Chavis's era became discouraged and emigrated to Sierra Leone or Liberia, newly established African lands for English or American blacks. But Chavis demonstrated that blacks could gain an education and win respect while staying in the United States. He also believed that Christians were to obey the civil laws and powers over them even when they believed those laws or powers were unjust. His own life demonstrated that belief. He never advocated or practiced disobedience of law or authority.

Chavis died in 1838 in his mid-seventies. Both history and posterity have been kind to this pioneer. In addition to recognition in books and journals for his early efforts in the fields of religion and education, a federal housing project and a recreational park in Raleigh, North Carolina, have been named for him. A marker placed near the site by the North Carolina Historical Society reads: "JOHN CHAVIS Early 19th Century Free Negro preacher and teacher of both races in North Carolina."

Suggestions for Further Reading

John Hope Franklin. *The Free Negro in North Carolina 1790-1860.* 1943. Reprint. New York: Russell & Russell, 1969. [See pp. 169-74 for the bulk of Franklin's discussion of Chavis.]

Noah Webster: Total Scholar

by Christa G. Habegger

*The Christian influence on American education has been pro-
found. The earliest text in America,* The New England Primer,
*taught students the alphabet with sentences such as "In Adam's
Fall We sinned all" and "Thy Life to mend, God's Book attend."
William McGuffey through his famous* Eclectic Readers *likewise
shaped the minds of children with the precepts of God's Word.
The name of a Christian educator that has survived the longest,
though, is Noah Webster.*

The student types a few words, hesitates, then reaches for his copy
of Webster's dictionary to check a word. Around the world wherever
English is spoken or studied, Webster is a household name. Everyone
knows Webster wrote a dictionary, although some people would confuse
author-Noah with orator-Daniel (a friend of Noah Webster, but no kin).
Some even recall reading Webster's famous Blue-Backed Speller. What
most people do not know is that Noah Webster was a great patriot,
economist, scientific researcher, agriculturist, humanitarian, and, especially, a Christian.

Noah Webster was born in Connecticut in 1758. His father was a
farmer who served as a deacon in the Congregational church. His mother,
Mercy, was a great-granddaughter of Governor William Bradford. The
couple reared five children, each of whom worked long and hard on the
family farm.

At fourteen Noah began a serious study of literature under the clergyman of his parish, and at sixteen he was admitted to Yale College. His
class, later recognized as the most brilliant Yale ever produced, included
in addition to Webster, a poet and minister to France, a United States
treasurer, judges and chief justices, and other men of influence in government. Their education at Yale was interrupted several times by the
Revolutionary War. During his junior year Noah and his two brothers
enlisted in a militia under his father's command.

Faith of Our Fathers: Scenes from American Church History

A veteran, Noah returned to college and graduated with honors in 1778. His education had only begun. He spent the rest of his long life amassing knowledge. His habits of personal study and thorough research enabled him to make outstanding contributions to learning in the United States.

After college and law study, Noah was eager to set up a legal practice in order to reimburse his father the large sum expended for his education. However, lawyers were plentiful and fees scarce, and Noah's prospects of success were bleak. He therefore established himself as a schoolteacher in his hometown.

As a teacher, he was frustrated by the state of elementary education in the country. Most school buildings were drafty, shabby structures, and textbooks were inadequate. Teachers, often ill-equipped for the job, made learning a tedious, rigid affair. Webster, on the other hand, proposed his philosophy that "the pupil should have nothing to discourage him." In addition to improving the quality of education in his own school, he began publishing essays in support of imaginative education.

One of the greatest dearths of eighteenth century education was in textbooks. Children learned to read from British primers which were largely archaic and promoted affected speech. The only other textbook was the Bible. Webster objected to the use of the Bible as a textbook, said one writer, because of "the tendency of children to treat with freedom, if not contempt, sacred names and objects. It was not so much his purpose to keep the Bible from children, as it was to increase their respect for it."

Following the Revolution, Americans were free from British controls in government only. In fashions and in literature they still depended exclusively on British tastes. Webster pioneered in producing textbooks which were peculiarly American in content, spelling, and word usage. His illustrations promoted American ideals and good moral principles. His *Grammatical Institute of the English Language*, popularly called the Blue-Backed Speller, became the basis for learning all over America. By the time he was twenty-five, Noah Webster was already known as the nation's schoolmaster.

Although his speller and other books were widely used, it would be a mistake to assume that Webster became wealthy or enjoyed universal approval. He printed many of his works at his own expense. Publishers of rival textbooks hurled abuse at him constantly, ridiculing his outrageous personal vanity in setting himself up as an authority.

The charge of vanity was made against Webster for more than sixty years. Regardless of the subject, he had strong, inflexible views which he propounded dogmatically. The public was often unready to accept the change, particularly at the suggestion of a man considered pompous and puritanical. Those who knew him best knew him as a modest, kindly, though serious, person, whose motives were noble and whose every energy was expended to serve God and country.

By the time Webster was thirty-one he had written volumes of provocative essays on education, authored schoolbooks, taught, practiced law, and edited a magazine. Despite his busy schedule, he had also found time to fall in love with Miss Rebecca Greenleaf of Boston. After a lengthy courtship, necessitated by Webster's financial insecurity, they were married on October 26, 1789. Noah wrote in his diary: "This day I became a husband. . . . I am united to an amiable woman, and, if I am not happy, shall be disappointed." He was not disappointed. Indeed, their marriage was a model of felicity. Rebecca was a lovely, soft-spoken, elegant woman who proved to be a wonderful companion, homemaker, and helpmate to her husband.

The newlyweds set up housekeeping in West Hartford. A friend remarked; "Webster has returned and brought with him a very pretty wife. I wish him success, but I doubt in the present decay of business in our profession whether his profits will enable him to keep up the style he sets out with. I fear he will breakfast upon Institutes, dine upon Dissertations, and go to bed supperless."

Between the publication of his textbooks and his famous dictionary, Noah Webster contributed to virtually every area of American thought, a few of which are the following:

- In 1783 Webster set a precedent for preserving American history with the publication of Governor John Winthrop's journal.
- Webster petitioned state legislatures to enact copyright laws giving authors exclusive rights to the publication of their works.
- Politically a Federalist (an advocate of a strong central union of the states and of the adoption of the U.S. Constitution), Webster was active all of his adult life either by holding office locally or by speaking out boldly in the press on the national level.
- On behalf of the Constitutional Convention which was in session in Philadelphia in 1787, Webster published *Examination of the Leading Principles of the Federal Constitution*.
- When American enthusiasts were rallying in support of involvement in the French Revolution, Webster penned influential essays in favor of the administration's policy of neutrality. To provide the public with news of developments, he published a daily paper in 1793, the first of its kind.
- Webster advocated a system of American banking and insurance, both new ideas at the time.
- In 1799 Webster published a massive work in two volumes containing the history of pestilential diseases around the world from every period of time.

Faith of Our Fathers: Scenes from American Church History

The number of Webster's achievements would seem to preclude his being much of a family man; however, he was the attentive head of his family, consisting of four daughters—his "angels"—and one son. His household operated, said one writer, "with perfect regularity and order, for *method* was the presiding principle of his life. In the government of his children there was but one rule, and that was instantaneous and entire obedience." Yet letters from his wife or quotations from his children reveal him to have been a most affectionate, tender father who understood the value of stern discipline balanced by parental love and protection.

The "nation's schoolmaster" was vitally interested in the schooling of his own children. A biographer wrote, "He therefore threw open his extensive library to his children at an early period in their lives, and said, in the words of Cotton Mather, 'Read, and you will know.' "

Always deeply religious and a staunch Calvinist in the Congregational church, Webster was nonetheless not a saved man until 1808, when he was fifty, during the Second Great Awakening. Under the ministry of the Reverend Moses Stuart, Dr. Webster began inquiring into the matter of personal faith and one's standing before God. His son-in-law, Chauncey A. Goodrich, recorded that Dr. Webster began studying the doctrines of the gospel with the result that "he felt that salvation *must* be wholly of grace. He felt constrained . . . to cast himself down before God, confess his sins, [and] implore pardon through the merits of the Redeemer." He then began his practice of Bible study and prayer which continued until his death. He publicly professed Christ in April 1808 along with two of his daughters.

By 1800 Webster had begun work on his dictionary, for which there was no real precedent, particularly not in America. He was not content to examine existing dictionaries, which were full of errors and careless scholarship. For years he immersed himself in the literature of other cultures, searching out links to English words, establishing etymologies and patterns in the language. By 1813 he knew twenty languages, later adding three others and several dialects of English and German. As preliminary work on his dictionary, Webster compiled a Synopsis, which required ten years of research. His method of study was this: "On a semicircular table . . . he placed his books; beginning at the right end of the table, he would thumb grammars and dictionaries while tracing a given word through the twenty languages, making notes of his discoveries."

Having exhausted the libraries of this country, he went to Europe to complete his research in June 1824. He was sixty-seven when he completed his dictionary. He wrote on that occasion: "I finished writing my dictionary in January, 1825, at my lodgings in Cambridge, England. When I had come to the last word, I was seized with a trembling, which made it somewhat difficult to hold my pen steady for writing." His excitement is understandable. To complete a dictionary of seventy thousand entries—

the next largest work being the old Johnson dictionary of twenty thousand fewer entries—was a monumental accomplishment. He had feared that he would not live to complete it.

Webster was a natural definer of words with a gift for explaining terms clearly. The dictionary, first published in two bulky volumes, was entitled *An American Dictionary of the English Language*. It received immediate acceptance. There was no doubt that Webster's dictionary was superior to all existing works. Soon it was standard in England as it already was in America. For the next several years, Webster continued to correct his entries and to add hundreds of others.

Webster lived to make one more outstanding contribution—the Amended Version of the King James Bible. He felt that "there were regrettable faults in the language [of the King James], . . . faults of grammar, of archaism, of geography, and of immodesty. These had long been deplored." Webster called this "the most important undertaking" of his career. With his customary thoroughness, Webster researched carefully, checking words in the original languages and correcting the flaws of the King James Version, many of which he acknowledged to be merely differences between the meaning of a word in 1611 and the meaning of the same word two hundred years later. Webster did not attempt to change the style of the King James Version, but rather to clarify meanings. He also reworded passages in which there were unnecessary vulgarities. On this subject Webster said, "Language which cannot be uttered in company without a violation of decorum or the rules of good breeding, exposes the scriptures to scoffs of unbelievers, impairs their authority, and multiplies or confirms the enemies of our holy religion."

A few examples of the type of change he made for clarity are these: he substituted *who* for *which* when the reference was to persons; *hinder* for *let; interest* for *usury;* and *cows* for *kine*. In I Corinthians 4:4, Webster changed "For I know nothing *by* myself," to the more nearly correct, "For I know nothing *against* myself."

Initially Webster's American Version did not gain acceptance. He wrote in 1835, "I do not know that any person has yet hazarded a commendation of the work." Later that year, however, the Yale faculty officially endorsed it, and from then on it was widely used throughout Connecticut.

Although his Bible was his crowning achievement, the aging scholar was not idle during his last years. He continued, as he was accustomed, to rise early and to spend hours in disciplined study. He revised his published works, visited with family and friends, and took long, brisk walks to maintain bodily health. One cool Monday in 1843 Webster walked twice to the post office, and on returning, felt chilled. By Friday, his lungs began to fill with fluid and on Sunday he spoke his willingness to meet his Saviour. "I'm ready to go," he said. "My work is all done; I know in whom I have believed," A few minutes before eight that evening he ceased to breathe. He was eighty-five.

A Yale scientist, Benjamin Silliman, wrote this tribute to Webster in his journal: "He died in the fulness of reputation, of health, of mental power, and of Christian faith. He has left a brilliant fame. Millions have been instructed by his writings, and millions more will study them in years to come. . . . His dictionary surpasses all others. . . . His elementary works for schools . . . and other works remain to instruct mankind."

Suggestions for Further Reading

Richard M. Rollins. *The Long Journey of Noah Webster*. University of Pennsylvania Press, 1980.

Jedediah Strong Smith

by Dayton Walker

Every American child in elementary school has read of the adventures of explorers such as Lewis and Clark and Zebulon Pike. These are the men responsible for blazing the trails that enabled Americans to push westward. Jedediah Strong Smith has not enjoyed the renown that these other explorers have known, but his contribution to western exploration is hardly negligible. In addition, despite being in a profession that was often marked by drunkenness, profanity, and sexual vice, Smith presented a sterling example of godly Christian character.

From a purely secular viewpoint, Jedediah Smith earned the right to a prominent place in American history. Packing a lifetime of pioneering achievement into a nine-year odyssey (1823-31), he opened the historic gateway to the Far West (South Pass); was the first reported white man to journey overland to California; the first to cross the treacherous Sierra Nevada range from the west; the first to travel across the arid Great Basin, north and south as well as east and west; and the first to negotiate the California coast north to Oregon. A trapper by trade, his 668 beaver pelts taken in the 1824-25 season may be the record for a single mountaineer. Venturing boldly into an area that was *terra incognita*, he came to know the West better than any other man alive. Historian Stephen W. Sears ranks Smith "beside Lewis and Clark," and biographer Dale Morgan labels him "an authentic American hero."

"Old Jed," as his mountain companions frequently referred to him, has failed to receive the recognition due him because his journals and maps were not made public until 1934. His writings, and those of his associates, reveal him to be an extraordinary trailblazer. In the midst of a free-spirited band known for its gross vices, Jedediah was grim, modest, and mild—"one who never smoked or chewed tobacco, never uttered a profane word." Smith, too, was indifferent to personal suffering, possessing, said one writer, "endurance beyond the point where other men died, courage and coolness under fire, intelligence that impressed

91

everyone, leadership of a high order, and energy and drive enough for three men.''

In a profession where gain and adventure were the primary objectives, Jedediah instead viewed his calling as a spiritual mission somewhat analogous to the journeys of the Apostle Paul. His letters evidence distress at the lack of Christian fellowship, sincere acknowledgement of both the sovereignty of God and the free will of man, accurate memorization of key Scripture passages such as John 3:16, and especially a concern for the welfare of his family and friends residing east of the Mississippi. Along with his rifle, skinning knife and whetstone, awl holder, bullet pouch, powder container, traps and trap sack, and pistols, Smith always carried his Bible, a collection of Wesleyan hymns (his background was Methodist), *Evidences of Christianity* by William Paley, a six-volume set of Matthew Henry's commentaries, a theological dictionary, and the works of Josephus. Trapper William Waldo commented, ''No one who knew him well doubted the sincerity of his piety.''

Jedediah was born January 6, 1799, the fourth of fourteen children of Jedediah and Sally Strong Smith. His parents were of God-fearing New England stock. Married in Easthampton, Connecticut, they had moved in the mid-1790s to Jericho (now Bainbridge), Chenango County, in the beautiful Susquehanna River Valley of south central New York.

In late 1810 or early 1811 the family pushed on to North East Township, Erie County, Pennsylvania. Young ''Diah'' there came under the influence of pioneer physician Dr. Titus Gordon Vespasian Simons. The doctor gave Jed a book on the travels of Lewis and Clark, a prophetic gift as it turned out. Next the Smiths settled in Ohio's Western Reserve, near Ashtabula, then on to Green Township in Ashland County.

At age twenty-three Jedediah answered an advertisement in the *St. Louis Missouri Gazette* for ''enterprising young men'' to join General William Ashley in the lucrative beaver trade. It was on this first expedition into the Black Hills of South Dakota that Jed almost met an early death.

Toward evening, the little company of men, threading their way through a narrow, brushy ravine, was surprised by a massive grizzly bear. Jedediah tried to run to open ground, but as he emerged from the thicket, he met the charging bear head on. The grizzly grabbed him around the middle, breaking Jed's knife and several of his ribs. The bear then bit down on Jed's head, laying the skull bare on one side close to his left eye and close to the right ear on the other. His left ear was almost completely torn away.

After the bear had been dispatched, Jedediah's friends stood around him wondering what to do. One would say, ''Come, take hold.'' And another would respond, ''Why not you?'' Finally, Smith himself told them what to do. He sent two men for water and asked James Clyman to sew him up as best as he could. Clyman later said of the incident,

"After stitching all the other wounds in the best way I was capable and according to Captain's [Smith's] direction, the ear being last, I told him I could do nothing for his ear. 'O, you must try to stitch it up some way or other,' said he. Then I put in my needle stitching it through and through and over and over, laying the lacerated parts together as nice as I could with my hands."

Smith bore the marks of this encounter for the rest of his life. His eyebrow had been torn away, his face scarred, and his ear torn and scarred. Until then, Jed had always kept his hair closely cropped and was cleanshaven in a time when most men wore beards. He continued to shave regularly, but he let his hair grow a little to try to cover up the scars.

The obvious leadership abilities of Diah led to a partnership with Ashley, then later with William Sublette and David E. Jackson. Smith-Sublette-Jackson dominated the American fur trade in the late 1820s; Jed, at twenty-seven, was the senior partner.

In 1826 Smith set out toward the southwest from the Cache Valley rendezvous above Utah's Great Salt Lake. Finding no beaver, Jedediah's party of fifteen entered what he called "a Country of Starvation." Crossing the Colorado River into northwestern Arizona, short of food and water, they providentially stumbled onto a settlement of hospitable Mojave Indians. Resupplied and told that California's Catholic missions were not far distant, the travelers ventured into the bleached desert. Fifteen days later they found San Gabriel, a refreshing contrast with its well-watered orchards of apples, peaches, oranges, and figs.

But California was Mexican territory; Jedediah was an illegal alien in a foreign country. His achievement of reaching the coast overland alarmed the California authorities, for they correctly foresaw the wave of American westward migration which would follow. While his men enjoyed the luxury of being guests at the mission, Smith was taken to San Diego for questioning by Governor-General Jose Maria de Echeandia. The Mexican leader assumed, naturally, that Smith and his party were spies; the journals Smith and clerk Harrison Rogers kept confirmed this to him. Jedediah escaped imprisonment only by the intercession of three American ship captains.

Smith's expedition spent the winter of 1826 in the San Joaquin Valley. Leaving most of the men in a camp on the Stanislaus River, Jed, Robert Evans, and Silas Gobel then made the historic crossing of the Sierra Nevada range. On the other side they nearly died in the torrid desert; yet Diah's calm perseverance enabled them to survive. On June 25, 1827, Evans's strength gave out. Temporarily abandoning him, Smith and Gobel continued in search of water. Three miles ahead they found some, then rushed back to save the life of Evans. Reaching the flooded Jordan River on the southern edge of the Great Salt Lake, Smith assembled a makeshift raft of reeds. Holding the tow rope between his teeth, Jedediah pulled the other two and their possessions across the current. When the trio arrived at the Bear Lake rendezvous July 3, a cannon salute greeted them, for they had long been given up as dead.

During these hazardous treks, Jed felt his keen need of Christian fellowship. He wrote often of his desire to retire from trapping and to join his family back in civilization. To his elder brother Ralph, Smith wrote, "I say, pray for me, my brother, and may He, before Whom not a sparrow falls without notice, bring us in His own good time, together again." He regularly sent money home, commenting that "Providence had made him steward of a small pittance, and his prayer was that while allowed the privilege of using it, he might use it without abuse."

Nothing is known of Jedediah's conversion, but his salvation can be clearly deduced from such statements as these: "How often ought we on our bended knees to offer up our grateful acknowledgements for the gift of His dear Son." "Then let us come forward with faith, nothing doubting, and He will most unquestionably hear us." "I find our Saviour ever entreating and wooing us, using the most endearing language and endeavoring by every means without compelling (for that would at once destroy our free agency), to bring us to Him that we may have life."

After a ten-day stay at Bear Lake, Jedediah set out to rejoin the men left behind in central California. He chose the southward route, despite its difficulties. This time, however, the Mojaves were in a hostile mood. As Smith's party of eighteen was rafting across the Colorado, the Indians attacked, killing ten men. The remaining eight had few supplies left, and, crossing the desert mostly at night, entered California. This time Jedediah was obviously an unwelcome intruder. Arrested and jailed, he met with a furious Governor Echeandia. Again, a diplomatic sea captain salvaged Jed's freedom.

Agreeing to leave Mexican California immediately and forever, Smith picked up his stranded men and headed north. The northern California terrain was rich in beaver but difficult for travel. Clerk Rogers, also a devout Christian, wrote on May 22, 1828, "Oh, God! May it please Thee . . . to still guide and protect us through this wilderness of doubt and fear."

On July 14 the party was at the confluence of the Umpqua and Smith (named for Jedediah) rivers on the Oregon coast. Smith and two others went ahead to scout, and while they were gone, a Umpqua Indian tribe massacred the trappers in camp. Only Arthur Black escaped. He was reunited with Diah and his companions in mid-August at Fort Vancouver, headquarters for the British Hudson Bay Company.

The Hudson Bay leader, George Simpson, helped Smith retaliate against the Indians, recovered many of his beaver furs and his precious journals, and then paid Jedediah a generous price for the skins. In return, Smith filled the Britishers in on his discoveries and drew them a map.

Jedediah Strong Smith

Tired of the continued threat of death and a life of desperate loneliness, Jed "retired" from his Rocky Mountain mission. He bought a house in St. Louis and began to prepare his invaluable maps and writings for publication. The trading urge beckoned strongly, though, and in 1831 Jedediah joined a caravan bound for Santa Fe. It should have been a routine journey, but the train was forced to break up in the dry plain between the Arkansas and Cimarron rivers. They had no water.

Jedediah and Thomas Fitzpatrick looked for the Cimarron bed. Reaching a spot where they might dig for water, Smith so instructed Fitzpatrick. Jed rode on three miles farther and found a pool of the precious liquid. At the same time, however, a war party of fifteen to twenty Comanches approached. Seeing no escape, the mountain man boldly rode up to the chief and tried to make peace signs. The Indians apparently did not understand or were uninterested. The Comanches fanned out away from Smith and tried to spook his horse. When their shouts frightened the steed and it reared, they fired, hitting Jedediah in the shoulder. He swung around and shot the Indian leader through the chest. Seconds later a dozen lances pierced Smith's flesh, and he died "with only his God for comfort in the desert."

One can only speculate what the future of the United States might have been had it not been for men like Jedediah Smith. Instead of being the "gateway to the West," St. Louis might have been our westernmost city! This country was built by such men of stamina, courage, and fortitude, men who were not afraid to face unknown frontiers, men who were willing to bear the hardships necessary to "enlarge our coasts."

Jedediah Strong Smith: an explorer, a fur trapper and a trader, and, most important, a Christian—a man of faith whose life was an outstanding example of the grace of God and a consistent witness to those about him. He was a rugged individual living among the roughest of scoundrels; yet he was possessed with tender, sensitive feelings, no doubt nurtured by his study of the Word of God. One of the last things he wrote, just a few months before his death, serves as a fitting epitaph. Quoting a poet, Jedediah penned:

> Lord, I believe a rest remains
> to all Thy people known;
> A rest where pure enjoyment reigns,
> and Thou art loved alone.

Suggestions for Further Reading

Dale L. Morgan. *Jedediah Smith and the Opening of the West.* Indianapolis: Bobbs-Merrill, 1953.

Alson J. Smith. *Men Against the Mountains: Jedediah Smith and the South West Expedition of 1826-1829.* New York: John Day Company, 1965.

Narcissa Whitman

by Susan Lindner Zimmerman

Western expansion was a major characteristic of American life between the Revolution and the Civil War. The desire for a nation stretching "from sea to shining sea"—sometimes called the Manifest ("Obvious") Destiny of the United States—pushed explorers and pioneers ever westward and brought the United States into conflict with Great Britain and outright war with Mexico (1846-1848). The leaders in the settlement of the Oregon Country were not land-hungry settlers, however, but dedicated missionaries, notably Marcus and Narcissa Whitman. Their accomplishments as missionaries were perhaps mixed, but their contribution to the growth of America was outstanding.

Few women would care to spend the first seven months of married life traveling three thousand miles, especially mounted sidesaddle for nearly two thousand of those miles. Few wives would want their first housekeeping venture to be in a homemade tent pitched on the prairie. And few brides would consent to share most of their honeymoon with another couple plus a motley crew of hired hands, curious Indians, and profane fur trappers.

Those who would say that Narcissa Prentiss Whitman made a sorry start in marriage might also label the remainder of this nineteenth-century Oregon missionary's life a failure. Her first home as a married woman was for three and one-half years a scantily furnished lean-to. Her only child drowned at the age of two. After her daughter's death, she became the often exhausted foster mother to sickly half-breed youngsters and orphans. In Oregon she never enjoyed the fellowship of a church or community as she had known in her beloved native New York. She never saw her family or in-laws after her trek west and rarely received mail. And only eleven years after Marcus and Narcissa Whitman began to minister to the Cayuse Indians at Waiilatpu, the "place of the rye grass," husband and wife were murdered by savages.

Yet by other standards Narcissa Whitman made a significant contribution to America's Christian heritage and to the westward expansion of a young United States. Narcissa's attitude toward her often unhappy circumstances is an impressive example of Christian piety. And she seems to have managed well the delicate balance between feminine dependence and independence so necessary for frontier women. In some areas of life, especially her mission work, she often failed; but this should not be allowed to obscure the illustration of God's mighty workings in the life of an ordinary wife and mother placed in a difficult situation.

"Waiting the Leading of Providence"

"I wish Narcissa would not always have so much company." Clarissa Prentiss made this lament perhaps after a harried evening of visitors at the Prentiss home, but the somewhat stern New England mother was probably secretly proud of her vivacious, popular eldest daughter. Born on March 14, 1808, at Prattsburg in western New York, Narcissa was a family as well as church and town favorite. Judge Stephen Prentiss, a comfortably situated carpenter, headed a cheerful, affectionate family. His third child of nine sons and daughters early displayed those qualities which later moved one of Marcus Whitman's minister associates to write that Narcissa was a "highly gifted, polished American lady."

Part of Narcissa's "polish" came from excellent education—public grade school in Prattsburg, study at church-sponsored, co-educational Franklin Academy, teacher training at Emma Willard's Female Seminary in Troy, New York, and considerable private reading of the Scriptures, Bunyan's *Pilgrim's Progress,* missionary biographies, and scholarly volumes of church history and theology. The Prentiss family was active in the Presbyterian church; their large home near the village square often hosted visiting evangelists and church elders. A feature of the frequent revival meetings as well as regular services was Narcissa's soprano voice—"as sweet and musical as a chime of bells."

Most important to Narcissa's preparation for life as a missionary doctor's wife was her conversion at the age of eleven during Prattsburg revival meetings in 1819. Her growth in the Lord Jesus Christ was evident, for at sixteen Narcissa dedicated herself to be a missionary. She reflected on this decision several years later: "I frequently desired to go to the heathen but only half-heartedly . . . it was not until the first Monday of Jan. 1824 that I felt to consecrate myself without reserve to the Missionary work waiting the leading of Providence concerning me."

"Waiting the leading of Providence" seemed to be one of Narcissa's special gifts during the eleven years between her missionary call and the coveted acceptance by the American Board of Commissioners for Foreign Missions. The young woman spent the latter part of those years teaching kindergarten in Bath, New York. She continued to be an active member of the Presbyterian church. During an evening service in Angelica, New York, Narcissa listened to Samuel Parker, a school teacher and preacher under missionary appointment, appeal for workers in Oregon. Twenty-six-year-old Narcissa approached Parker with a thoughtful question: Would the American Board accept an "unmarried female" for the Oregon mission?

Narcissa's 1834 offer to Samuel Parker is a fine counter to the myth that the mission field is merely a retreat for dull, unattractive "spinsters." Friends described the golden-haired singer as "symmetrically formed, very graceful in her voice and carriage . . . with a brilliant sparkling eye—peculiarly so when engaged in animated conversation." Beyond these personal attributes, Narcissa was remarkable for the genuine dedication sparking her desire. When Parker wrote to the board on December 17, 1834, he reported that Miss Prentiss was "very anxious to go to the heathen. Her education is good—piety conspicuous—her influence good."

The American Board could not be persuaded to send an "unmarried female" across the continent to a frontier mission, or to any mission for that matter. Narcissa was left to continue "waiting the leading of Providence."

On February 23, 1835, Narcissa wrote the American Board: "Having obtained favour of the Lord and desiring to live for conversion of the world, I now offer myself to the American Board to be employed in their service among the heathen, if counted worthy." She included references from three ministers. One mentioned in a postscript that Narcissa was to "hereafter become the companion of Doctor Marcus Whitman."

While the exact circumstances of Narcissa's first acquaintance with the thirty-two-year-old doctor are uncertain, their marriage was definitely not, as one Whitman biographer suggests, "a most extraordinary turn of fate." The Lord used their common association with the New York area Presbyterian churches and probably the tactful matchmaking of both younger sister Jane Prentiss and Samuel Parker to bring together a man and a woman who both expressed interest in Oregon missions definitely before their engagement, if not before their meeting.

On the Oregon Trail

> *In the deserts let me labor,*
> *On the mountains let me tell,*
> *How He died—the blessed Saviour—*
> *To release a world from hell!*
> *Let me hasten,*
> *Far in heathen lands to dwell.*

Narcissa's clear soprano was the only voice still singing during the final stanza of the last hymn at her wedding. Later the family and wedding guests were understandably choked with emotions as the bride, attired in her best black bombazine, prepared to leave with her husband on the honeymoon trek to Oregon.

The Whitman pilgrimage west is as important a part of Narcissa's story as the mission she later helped her husband establish. Along with her companion, missionary wife Eliza Spalding, Narcissa was one of the first white women to cross the Rocky Mountains. The journal and letters Narcissa wrote during her trip demonstrate her unswerving trust in her husband, her enthusiastic pioneering spirit, and her unquestioning faith in God.

Marcus Whitman was neither stupid nor foolhardy, but he was stubborn. The advice he received while considering his unusual wedding journey likely resembled that of George Catlin, artist and seasoned western traveler: "[I would not take] a white female into that country for the whole continent of America." But Whitman, after an 1835 trial journey to the Rockies with the America Fur Company caravan, rightly concluded that "where wagons could go, women could go." A wagon had never yet rumbled all the way to Oregon, but the doctor was determined to try—with both the wagon and the woman.

Before embarking on her steamboat voyage up the Missouri River, the new bride wrote her parents that she had "one of the kindest Husbands and the very best every way." A few days later, as the missionaries drew closer to the start of overland travel at Liberty, Missouri, Narcissa paid Marcus a worthy compliment: "I have such a good place to shelter, under my husband's wings. . . . I love to confide in his judgement and act under him." On the last leg of the journey in eastern Oregon, the tired, now pregnant wife wrote: "My husband who is one of the best the world ever knew is always ready to provide a comfortable shade." She had spent nearly seven months watching and helping Marcus contend with sick companions, frustrating delays, a slow-moving cattle herd, and an unwieldly wagon. Marcus had to leave his wagon—reduced to a two-wheeled cart—at Fort Boise before crossing the Blue Mountains. But he brought his wife safely to a home in Oregon.

Narcissa rarely burdened Marcus with complaints or shirked her own travel duties. She usually approached difficult experiences with a spirit of adventure. The new wife happily baked bread on the prairie—"awkward work to bake at first out of doors, but we have become so accustomed to [it] now we do it very easy." When the mission party joined the fur company wagons near the Loup Fork of the Platte River, Narcissa quickly adjusted to the traders' grueling travel schedule: "Start usually at six—travel till eleven, encamp, rest and feed, start again about two—travel until six or before . . . then encamp for the night." When the caravan reached buffalo country and the diet became "meat and tea in the morn and tea and meat at noon," Narcissa reported. "I relish it well and it agrees with me . . . so long as I have buffalo meat I do not wish anything else.''

As the journey wore on there were times when the traveler confided various hardships to her journal. She craved a piece of ''Ma's bread'' or dreamed that ''pork and potatoes would relish extremely well.'' By August the heat grew so oppressive that Narcissa exclaimed: ''Truly I thought 'the Heavens over us were brass, & the earth iron under our feet' '' (a reference to Deuteronomy 28:32). Her longing for privacy grew especially keen. After months of sleeping in a crowded tent, Narcissa's impression of primitive Fort Hall was ''Anything that looks like a house makes us glad.''

Yet Narcissa's comments on the difficulties of the Oregon Trail do not smack of self-pity. She drew enduring strength from her relationship with the Lord Jesus Christ. During a particularly fatiguing trek between Green River and Fort Hall, Narcissa stated: ''It is good to feel that he is all I want, & all my righteousness, & if I had ten thousand lives I would give them all to him.'' When the young woman was weary from the scorching heat or restless from long hours perched on her horse, she remembered that ''the Lord is better to us than our fears. I always find it so.''

"Far in Heathen Lands to Dwell"

''Jane if you want to be happy, get a good husband as I have got and be a missionary,'' Narcissa wrote to her younger sister not quite two months after her marriage. Had Jane talked with her sister years later, she would have received the same encouragement about the husband, but a more seasoned Narcissa may have tempered the ''be a missionary'' with practical suggestions for dealing with primitive living conditions, inscrutable natives, and difficult co-workers.

The physical drudgery involved in building a mission nearly broke Marcus and Narcissa's health. After settling his wife in a makeshift dwelling, Marcus became farmer, butcher, dairyman, lumberjack, and carpenter, as well as missionary physician and teacher. Narcissa took up the duties of frontier housewife, which included cooking over an open fireplace and trying to finish her home's rough interior.

But these time-consuming duties seemed a minor problem compared to the Whitman's uneasy relationship with the Cayuse. Narcissa anguished over keeping house under the eyes of curious Indians, who unreservedly walked in and out of the Whitman dwelling. She opened her heart to her mother: ''The greatest trial to a woman's feelings is to have her cooking and eating room always filled with four or five or more Indians—men—especially at meal time. . . . They are so filthy they make a great deal of cleaning wherever they go, and this wears out a woman very fast.'' Most heartbreaking was the Indians' reaction to ''Husband's'' preaching: ''They feel so bad, disappointed, and some of them angry, because husband tells them that they are all of them in the broad road to destruction, and that worshipping will not save them. They try to persuade him not to talk such bad talk to them . . . but talk good talk, or tell some story, or history, so that they may have some Scripture names to learn.''

Temporary respite from the Cayuse hostility came with the birth of a beautiful, blue-eyed daughter, Alice Clarissa, on Narcissa's twenty-ninth birthday. The Indians, even the suspicious chiefs, thronged Narcissa's room to see ''Cause Te-mi'' (Cayuse girl). Alice was a healthy child and her mother's almost constant companion, especially when Marcus was away on frequent doctoring jaunts or trips to Walla Walla for supplies. The child chattered in both Nez Perce and English and learned to sing, loving especially ''Rock of Ages.''

Sunday afternoon, June 23, 1839, Marcus and Narcissa were enjoying some rare leisure reading before dinner. Their toddler daughter slipped from the room with two cups, chirping, ''Supper is almost ready; let Alice get some water.'' A short time later Narcissa sent her half-breed helper, Margaret, outside to check on Alice. When Margaret returned unable to find the youngster, the parents hurried outside—and saw two cups floating on the river. Marcus applied artificial respiration to the still form an Indian finally pulled from the water, but little Alice Clarissa was already lifeless.

The sorrowing parents accepted the tragedy as the will of the Lord, even as an aid to their missionary difficulties. August of 1838 had seen the arrival of four new missionary couples and a single man seeking temporary shelter at Waiilatpu before settling new missions in the Oregon country. The visit for seven of the new workers stretched through the winter of 1838-1839 and proved to be a miserable sojourn. It was nearly impossible for twelve people, including a baby and two young children, to live comfortably in a lean-to. Personality and policy differences swiftly grew bitter.

The differences grew sharper at mission meetings attended by Henry Spalding from his station at Lapwai Creek. The New York-born minister held a long-standing grudge against Whitman based on his fury at Narcissa for rejecting a long-ago marriage proposal. But Narcissa recognized that the death of Alice soon mellowed bitterness: ''The death of our babe had a great affect upon all in the mission; it softened their hearts towards us, even Mr. S's for a season.''

Alice's drowning may also have softened the Indian's hearts for a season, but any kindness was short-lived. The great westward migration to Oregon was growing steadily, and the Cayuse feared the incursion of the white man. Waiilatpu was a strategic stopping place not only for additional missionaries, but also for settlers pushing towards the Willamette

Valley, for trappers and fur traders, artists and naturalists. The Whitmans opened their home to all, including numerous foster children.

To the weary white immigrants, Narcissa was a gracious hostess; to the Cayuse, she was a haughty lady who preferred the companionship of her own people to that of the natives. The mission station—now graced by a frame house, several farm buildings, and cultivated fields— had become a bitter symbol of white man's prosperity. Hostility to Marcus grew as well, finally peaking when he was unable to stanch a measles epidemic which ravaged the tribe.

On Monday afternoon, November 29, 1847, the hostility of the Indians burst forth in a sudden massacre which claimed Marcus and Narcissa along with twelve others. The Cayuse later burned the mission station, and the tough, waving rye grass gradually choked the plowed fields.

Epilogue

"Mrs. Whitman was not adapted to savage but civilized life. She would have done honor to her sex in a polished and exalted sphere. The natives esteemed her proud. . . . It was her *misfortune*, not her *fault*. She was adapted to a different destiny," the Reverend H.K.W. Perkins, missionary at The Dalles, Oregon, wrote to Jane Prentiss to explain the massacre. From his close association with both Marcus and Narcissa, he claimed that neither was suited to be a missionary.

Perhaps so. Perkins's contention is difficult to resolve, for though the Whitmans failed to balance the opposing forces of Indian need and immigrant need, they died trying. But the Methodist missionary erred in one analysis of Narcissa. She *did* do "honor to her sex"—in a rough-and-tumble sphere.

Despite incredible pressures during nearly twelve years of marriage, Narcissa maintained a close, loving relationship with her husband. When Marcus journeyed to Boston to intercede for the Oregon mission with the American Board, Narcissa sorely missed his companionship. She wrote her in-laws: "His society was my life, and while I had him I never knew that I was lonely." Bereaved of her daughter, she became a compassionate mother to the dirty, ill-clad, often sick youngsters thrust upon her. Three of her adopted orphans later remembered a Narcissa who taught them to garden and took them on horseback rides and picnics. And despite her primitive surroundings, there is ample evidence that Narcissa did her best to make her house a reasonably comfortable and attractive home. Thousands of miles from eastern civilization, the dwelling at Waiilatpu contained such refinements as rocking chairs, bookcases, mirrors, and china. In addition to being wife and mother, Narcissa taught school to a wide assortment of children during her early missionary years. Native women came to her home for sewing and weaving classes. She entranced the Indians with her singing. And she left Americans a volume of richly detailed letters offering a glimpse into pioneer life.

Narcissa once wrote her parents: "The missionary work is hard, up-hill work, even the best of it. There are no flowery beds of ease here." It is safe to assume that even if Narcissa was not *perfectly* suited to the life of an Oregon missionary, she hardly would have adorned a flowery bed of ease. This realistic pioneer woman knew that the strength for "up-hill work" comes only from the God who appoints the work.

Suggestions for Further Reading

Clifford Merrill Drury, ed. *First White Women over the Rockies.* Vol. 1. Glendale, Calif.: Arthur H. Clark Company, 1963. [Pages 25-170 contain extensive selections from Narcissa Whitman's diary and letters.]

Nard Jones. *The Great Command: The Story of Marcus and Narcissa Whitman and the Oregon Country Pioneers.* Boston: Little, Brown and Company, 1959.

Ruth A. Tucker. *From Jerusalem to Irian Jaya: A Biographical History of Christian Missions.* Grand Rapids: Zondervan, 1983. [See pp. 97-104.]

Samuel F.B. Morse:
Christian Inventor

by George Mulfinger, Jr.

The period between the Revolution and the Civil War was an inventive age. Eli Whitney with his cotton gin, Samuel Colt with his repeating revolver, John Deere with steel-edged plow, and numerous others contributed to the advance of American technology. Christians were a part of this inventive surge too. Cyrus McCormick, for example, took the enormous profits he made from the horse-drawn reapers he manufactured and gave liberally to Christian organizations and causes. Possibly the most important invention of the era, the telegraph, was also the work of a Christian, Samuel F.B. Morse.

Samuel Finley Breese Morse (1791-1872) was without doubt one of the most versatile geniuses this country has produced. Dubbed "The American Leonardo da Vinci" by a leading biographer, he was an artist, an inventor, a college professor, and a writer. Moreover, and not as widely known, he was an exemplary Christian who pursued his varied endeavors to the glory of God.

Morse's artistic abilities were apparent early in his life. At age four, he scratched a portrait into a neighbor's chest of drawers with a pin. The lady of the house soon made her dissatisfaction painfully clear to young "Finley."

Though his father was the town pastor, Finley was not noted for his good conduct. When he was seven his parents sought to help him by sending him to a Christian school founded for the purpose of promoting "true piety and virtue." The only records that remain of his scholastic endeavors there are those of his demerits: eight in spelling and eighteen for whispering. To encourage better behavior, his parents offered all manner of inducements; cakes, pies, books, and vacations from school work, but in the long run it was their insistence on daily prayer and Bible study that benefited him most.

Samuel F.B. Morse: Christian Inventor

The next phase of his education took him to Yale College. There in his spare time he decorated the walls of his dormitory room with a mural depicting "struggling collegians climbing the hill of science." In his junior year, art became a more serious part of his life. A freshman offered to sit for a portrait. Morse captured his likeness so successfully that other students were soon paying for his services. His reputation as a portrait artist spread, and during the remainder of his stay at Yale he was liberally supplied with commissions.

The year following his graduation, Morse became a pupil of the noted painter and author Washington Allston. Morse accompanied Allston to England, where Morse was introduced to Benjamin West, the most respected personage in the world of art at that time. The friendship that ensued from that meeting proved to be a vital link in Morse's chain of success, for it was West who instilled in Morse the mental discipline that he so sorely needed.

On one occasion Morse appeared at the West mansion to display his latest drawing for the master painter. Fortunately for Morse, West's fondness for him in no way inhibited his frankness. His comment was simply, "Very good; now take it home and finish it." He pointed out the omissions, and Morse dutifully went back to his studio to add the missing ingredients.

After three attempts to polish his work, Morse began to realize that he had been existing in a world of mediocrity. West skillfully filled in the gaps in his technique; before his four-year sojourn abroad had ended, Morse had taken his place alongside West's most gifted pupils—men such as Gilbert Stuart, Rembrandt Peale, and John Trumbull.

While in England Morse came under the influence of William Wilberforce and his zealous group of evangelical Christians known as the Clapham Sect. Morse was thoroughly impressed with Wilberforce and stated, "What I saw of him in private gave me the most exalted opinion of him as a Christian." The testimony of these godly men soon brought Morse himself to accept Christ as his Saviour. The exact time of his conversion is not known, but on returning to the States he lost no time in coming forward in his own church and making a public profession of his faith.

The next few years found him busily engaged in painting portraits. During this period of his life, he painted such notables as President James Monroe, Noah Webster (the portrait used in the frontispiece for Webster's Dictionary), and General Lafayette.

While working in Concord, New Hampshire, he met his bride-to-be, Lucretia Pickering Walker. During their prolonged courtship his unrelenting efforts to win her to the Lord eventually bore fruit when she also came to trust Christ as her Saviour. Theirs was a happy Christian home, marred only by his necessary absences and the financial hardships that accompanied his work as an artist. But in spite of lean times he was able to say, "I feel satisfied that whilst engaged for God He will not suffer me to want."

Once again Europe beckoned. This time he desired to study the great masters of Italy and France. While in Paris he became intrigued with the French semaphore system of communication. Signals were relayed from mountaintop to mountaintop across the land by means of several arms pivoted in varying positions on the top of a pole. How much better was this, he thought, than the mail system back home. But the French semaphore system was still too slow. To a friend he remarked rather cryptically, "The lightning would serve us better." He was, of course, envisioning the use of electricity as a medium of communication.

During his return voyage to America, a specific plan of attack crystallized in his mind. He discussed his idea with several of the travelers in his group. Their exchange of ideas stimulated his thinking. He was no stranger to the world of electricity; he had experimented with voltaic cells at Yale shortly after their invention and had been a close friend of James Dana, an authority on electromagnetism and a pioneer in the use of the horseshoe electromagnet in this country. Now Morse's own creative genius had been fired. When he disembarked in New York Harbor, his notebook contained sketches of the first crude electric telegraph.

Providentially he received an appointment as professor of sculpture and painting at the University of the City of New York (later called New York University). This afforded him a place to experiment and served as a means of attracting those who were to become his assistants.

But there was no one to help him until his invention first showed unmistakable signs of promise. It was hard, lonely work those first few months. Although testing and development had to be carried out on a shoestring budget, Morse soon began to demonstrate his collection of voltaic cells, coils, and wires for his colleagues at the university with increasing confidence. People were skeptical, but none could deny that messages were being sent successfully from one side of the room to the other.

Soon Morse began to seek out individuals who would make capable assistants. The first to join him was Leonard Gale, a geology professor at the university. Gale advised Morse concerning battery voltage and currents and assisted in determining the number of turns to use on the electromagnets.

Next to join the group was Alfred Vail, a recent graduate of the university. Morse took an immediate liking to Vail; they shared the same beliefs and attended the same church. Vail provided the financial assistance to set up a model telegraph for demonstration purposes; the system was ultimately to aid them in securing a patent.

One of the earliest public demonstrations took place in Vail's hometown, Morristown, New Jersey. The sender and receiver were both at the same location, but the signals traversed some two miles of coiled wire between the two units. The spectators were enthusiastic, and the Morristown *Jerseyman* praised Professor Morse and his invention extravagantly.

In 1838 Morse and Vail gave a demonstration at the Franklin Institute in Philadelphia. Again the equipment functioned successfully and a favorable report was issued—the first acclaim to be received from representatives of the scientific world.

The next demonstration was in Washington. It was their fond hope to secure funds for a trial line between two major cities some distance apart. Among those witnessing the demonstrations were President Van Buren and several members of his cabinet. Congressman Francis O. J. Smith, chairman of the Committee on Commerce, was so impressed that he immediately wanted to become associated with Morse and his co-workers. Thus it was that there were four men in partnership when the American patent was finally granted in 1840—Morse, Gale, Vail, and Smith.

Several years were to pass before Congress would take action on their appropriation. In the meantime Morse attempted to secure English and French patents. His failure to impress the British officials with the practicality of his invention was more than offset by his spectacular success in Paris when he exhibited the telegraph before the French Academy of Sciences. Those who saw it were warmly enthusiastic, and he experienced little trouble in obtaining a French patent. Parisian newspapers called Morse one of the two greatest inventors of the age, the other being Daguerre, who had just perfected the world's first photographic process.

Late in 1842 Morse set up a demonstration line between the rooms of the House Committee on Commerce and the Senate Committee on Naval Affairs. Faithfully he remained on duty by his equipment, sending sample messages for the legislators and answering their questions. By the end of the year the Committee on Commerce had submitted a favorable report, and the chairman of the committee recommended that $30,000 be appropriated to set up an intercity telegraph system. The resolution passed both houses of Congress in March of 1843.

In addition to the appropriation for materials, Morse was placed on a government salary as superintendent of the project; Gale, Vail, and Professor James Fisher of New York University were hired as assistant superintendents. Smith donated his services as a legal advisor. Ezra Cornell, then a little-known plow salesman, was engaged to supervise the details of laying the underground cable.

When approximately nine miles of cable had been completed, Vail discovered defects in the insulation. Signals transmitted through the cable would undoubtedly be short-circuited before reaching their destination. The entire project faltered. Fisher was dismissed for incompetence; Gale resigned. Twenty-three thousand dollars of the appropriation had already been spent, seemingly for naught.

Smith suggested that Morse submit dishonest bills to Washington to obtain more funds. Morse flatly refused, saying, "I cannot consistently with any consideration of honor ask the Secretary of Treasury to approve an agreement which violates truth on the face of it." Because Morse was unwilling to compromise in any way, Smith too parted company with the group. Only Morse and Vail now remained, held together by the common bond of their Christian faith.

Winter had now come upon them, and nothing further could have been done even if they had known the next step. During the next few weeks much time was spent in searching libraries for ideas. From what he found in the literature, Vail was led to believe that the best solution would be to place the wires on poles. Spacing them every two hundred feet, only twenty-seven poles would be required for each mile.

Morse saw the wisdom of the plan. As soon as weather permitted, the cable was dug up and the wires were salvaged from it. The pipes encasing the wires were sold. Several hundred poles were quickly erected, and the wires were strung between them using the necks of broken bottles for insulators.

It was May 24, 1844. Morse had terminated the Washington end of the line in the Supreme Court chamber of the Capitol Building. Vail was ready in Baltimore. An appropriate portion of Scripture had been chosen for the occasion: "What hath God wrought!" (Num. 23:23). Morse transmitted the words slowly and accurately, requiring a full minute to complete the sentence. Almost immediately the identical words came back from Vail in Baltimore and registered on paper tape for all to see. It was a great moment of triumph for the inventor.

Immediately following this momentous occasion, no fewer than sixty-two individuals claimed to have invented the telegraph before Morse. Several of them began pirating his rights and erecting lines of their own. Frequently he was required to defend his patent rights in court. Although he almost invariably emerged victorious from his legal encounters, there were times of great anguish. The best remedy of such times of testing, he found, was reading from Psalm 37: "Fret not thyself because of evildoers, neither be thou envious against the workers of iniquity."

In time he received all the remuneration and honor that were rightfully his. For many years a forceful writer for the cause of orthodoxy and conservativism, he was now able to assist with generous contributions to all those organizations that were so dear to his heart—the American Tract Society, the American Bible Society, the City Mission Society in New York, the American and Foreign Christian Union, and many others. He assisted several churches with their building programs and was instrumental in founding at least two Christian colleges.

Samuel F.B. Morse: Christian Inventor

Morse was decorated by the sovereigns of Austria, Denmark, France, Italy, Portugal, Prussia, Spain, Turkey, and Württemburg. To demonstrate their appreciation, ten European nations joined in awarding him a gratuity of $60,000. Yet he never lost sight of eternal matters in the glitter of worldly acclaim. After attending a great banquet at which Napoleon III had shown him special honor, he wrote home to his brother Sidney, "And after all, of what account is it except to confirm the wisdom of Solomon in his utterance of 'All is vanity and vexation of spirit'? I make this reflection not in a cynical or ascetic spirit, but in view of the better things laid up for those who love God, and whose crowns and treasures are not the perishing temporary baubles of earth."

Suggestions for Further Reading
Oliver W. Larkin. *Samuel F.B. Morse and American Democratic Art.* Boston: Little, Brown and Company, 1954.

The Prayer Meetings That Changed the Nation

by Craig Jennings

Sometimes overlooked in the 1850s in America's harrowing rush toward the Civil War is what has rightly been called America's "Third Great Awakening." The Prayer Meeting Revival was much shorter in duration than the First or Second Great Awakenings, but in that brief period of less than two years it altered the course of American history.

America was in desperate need of revival in 1857. The volatile issue of slavery had exploded into open violence and an apprehensive country was on the brink of civil war. The booming American economy had ground to a halt due to a financial crisis that year. Railroad construction halted, factories shut down, banks failed, and thousands were unemployed. Most important, however, spiritual lethargy and declension permeated both churches and educational institutions where infidelity in the form of Unitarianism and transcendentalism was on the rise. Yet in the midst of this political, economic, and spiritual confusion, God sent revival.

The revival itself began in a very unpretentious manner in New York City. The North Reformed Dutch Church began a full-time program of evangelism to reach the people in the heart of the city—a section which most of the other churches had neglected. The church board employed a man by the name of Jeremiah C. Lanphier to work in the neighborhood as a full-time lay missionary. Mr. Lanphier resigned his regular job, and on July 1, 1857, he began his efforts through personal visitation. To further encourage visitors to come to the Sunday services, he placed posters in various hotels and boarding houses advertising the church. The Lord blessed his work, but Mr. Lanphier constantly battled discouragement. As he laid his burdens upon the Lord, however, he found comfort and strength. One day, after about two months of diligent work and prayer, Mr. Lanphier decided to invite other interested Christians to meet with him for prayer and mutual encouragement.

The Prayer Meetings That Changed the Nation

Accordingly, Lanphier announced that on September 23 there would be a prayer meeting at the noon hour for those who would like to gather with him and pray. Signs and handbills were printed announcing the meeting, but at noon on September 23, no one showed up at the church. Mr. Lanphier sat and waited, and finally after about half an hour one man came. By 1:00 P.M. when the meeting closed there were six people present. The next week twenty people came, and the third week there were forty people in attendance. At the third meeting those present decided to meet on a daily basis for prayer, and within four months the building adjoining the church was crowded to overflowing with three simultaneous meetings. The Plymouth Church in Brooklyn was soon opened for prayer, and by spring of 1858 there were at least twenty noon prayer meetings in New York City. Prayer meetings were soon started at other hours and preaching services were also inaugurated.

Soon other cities experienced revival. Prayer meetings were begun in November of 1857 at the Union Methodist Church in Philadelphia. A large auditorium was finally put into use where for many weeks over three thousand met for prayer day after day. There was hardly a city in the North where the influence of the revival was not felt, and revival soon spread to the South.

The prayer services in all the cities were conducted in a similar fashion. They began promptly at noon and ended promptly at 1:00 P.M. No one had to come for the entire time, but people were free to come and go as they chose. The service usually opened with a verse or two of a hymn and then the leader of the meeting prayed. Following this, anyone might give a testimony, pray, give a prayer request, or lead in a verse of a hymn. A time limit of five minutes was allowed per person, and the leader would ring a small bell if someone went overtime. That person would then have to stop and allow someone else to participate. At precisely 1:00 P.M. the leader would rise, pronounce the benediction, and dismiss the people. A few ministers would remain afterwards to counsel with those desiring spiritual help. As Charles Finney said, ''There was such a general confidence in the prevalence of prayer, that the people very extensively seemed to prefer meetings for prayer to meetings for preaching. The general impression seemed to be, 'We have had instruction until we are hardened; it is time for us to pray.' ''

As the revival spread, stories of conversions were spread across the front pages of numerous daily newspapers, which in turn stimulated increasing interest and participation in the prayer services. Even telegraph companies set aside certain hours in which businessmen could wire free of charge to other cities asking and giving information on the progress of the revivals. When the year-and-a-half revival subsided, it is estimated that over five hundred thousand and perhaps as many as a million people were converted, and that at the height of the revival (a six- to eight-week period) there were as many as fifty thousand persons converted every week throughout the country. It was even reported that some of the towns in New England did not have a single unconverted person.

However, the results and the significance of those short months of revival go beyond the glorious personal conversions. Perhaps the most significant aspect of these prayer meetings is that they were instituted and directed by laymen. The training afforded in these prayer meetings prepared many strong laymen to take active leadership roles in the church. Many good pastors, of course, supported these prayer meetings, but few were active organizing leaders.

Second, the spiritual strength gained from genuine revival prepared the country for the shock and sorrows of war on the field of battle and on the home front. During the Civil War, revival swept the Confederate army, encouraged by Christian generals such as Stonewall Jackson and Robert E. Lee. By the end of the war, 150,000 soldiers had been converted, and these conversions helped ease the feelings of hatred and bitterness which Reconstruction would bring. Revivals which broke out among blacks in 1858-59 prevented bloody slave uprisings which might otherwise have occurred.

Third, the revival inaugurated the largest outlay of money for philanthropic and Christian causes that America had ever experienced. Those whose lives were changed went on to found Christian schools and relief agencies and to support foreign missions. By the end of the century, the contributions of these new believers amounted to millions of dollars.

Considered as a whole, there can be no doubt that this revival of 1857-58 was the hand of God. Its original purpose was not the conversion of sinners but rather the spiritual relaxation and refreshment of weary saints in the duties and pressures of life. No well-known evangelists, extended preaching campaigns, or spectacular attractions drew people to the prayer meetings; in fact, there was no pressure or human leadership which brought the people together; it was only the gentle moving of God's Spirit. From the timing of the revival to the nature of the conversions, the power of God was clearly manifested, and all was accomplished through the much neglected medium of prayer.

Suggestions for Further Reading

Keith J. Hardman. "The Time for Prayer: The Third Great Awakening." *Christian History*, vol. 8, no. 3 (1989), pp. 32-34.

J. Edwin Orr. *The Fervent Prayer: The Worldwide Impact of the Great Awakening of 1858.* Chicago: Moody, 1974. [See pp. 1-44 in particular.]

Timothy L. Smith. *Revivalism and Social Reform.* New York: Abingdon, 1957. [Chapter 4 (pp. 63-79) sketches the course of the Prayer Meeting Revival.]

Robert E. Lee:
Christian, Soldier, Gentleman

by Craig Jennings

God often brings blessing out of tragedy. Certainly, little in American history appears as tragic as the Civil War, the clash of section against section, state against state, and sometimes literally brother against brother. Yet God in His sovereignty used the wrath of men to His own praise. Revivals swept through the ranks of both the blue and the gray. Outstanding Christians served in both armies: General Stonewall Jackson of the South; Admiral Andrew Foote, commander of U.S. Grant's gunboat fleet on the Missis-sippi; and Union General Oliver O. Howard (the man who General William Sherman said "runs the religion of this army") are out-standing examples. Perhaps the most respected of these leaders, though, was the gentle cavalier of Virginia, Robert Edward Lee.

"I am nothing but a poor sinner, trusting in Christ alone for salva-tion." These words which were spoken in 1864 came from the lips of one of America's most beloved citizens. Although involved in a losing cause, this man clearly exemplified the rare qualities of courage, devo-tion to duty, and honor. During his forty years of military service, he lived by Christian principles, and all who knew him had the highest respect for his integrity. This outstanding American was Robert E. Lee (1807-1870), the general who courageously led the Confederate forces during the American Civil War (1861-1865).

Robert E. Lee came from a long line of distinguished Americans. One of his ancestors had been the royal governor of Virginia, and his father had been a general in the American Revolution. Following in his father's footsteps, young Lee embarked on a military career himself. In 1829 he graduated with high honors from West Point and first served as a second lieutenant in the Corps of Engineers. Over the next thirty years, Lee continually proved his abilities on the battlefield and won several promotions. In spite of his accomplishments, however, Lee would be a forgotten man today if it were not for the crucial part he played in the Civil War.

By 1861 the bitter sectional rivalry between North and South could no longer be contained. One by one, seven Southern states voted themselves out of the Union and established the Confederate States of America, to be joined shortly thereafter by four other states. As the dark clouds of war gathered on the horizon, President Lincoln offered Lee the command of all United States forces. Lee now faced one of the most important decisions in his life. On the one hand he opposed slavery and did not believe that any state had the right to leave the Union. On the other hand Lee not only remained fiercely loyal to his native state of Virginia, but he also believed the North was unconstitutionally trying to force its will on the South. After much prayer, he made his decision. In a letter to his sister he wrote, "In my own person I had to meet the question whether I should take part against my native state. With all my devotion to the Union, and the feeling of loyalty and duty of an American citizen, I have not been able to make up my mind to raise my hand against my relatives, my children, my home. I have therefore resigned my commission in the army." On April 12, 1861, one week after Lincoln's offer, war broke out.

Over the next four years, Lee served as commander of the Army of Northern Virginia and as the chief military advisor to Jefferson Davis, the president of the Confederate States. As in the past, Lee fully carried out his new responsibilities, relying upon daily prayer to sustain him. He won a number of major victories even though his army was frequently outnumbered and short of supplies. Taking no credit for the early success of the Confederate cause, Lee warned his men against boasting in their own strength and reminded them that it was only God's mercy which sustained them.

Throughout the whole war, one of Lee's primary concerns was the souls of his men. He was always interested in the work of his chaplains and did everything in his power to make their task easier. For example, on Sundays he allowed only a minimum of military activity so that the soldiers would be able to attend church services. The spiritual leadership exercised by Lee and the other Christians in the army was so significant that one of the chaplains who had been with Lee throughout the entire war wrote that "any history of that army which omits an account of the wonderful influence of religion upon it—which fails to tell how the courage, discipline, and morale of the whole was influenced by the humble piety and evangelical zeal of many of its officers and men— would be incomplete and unsatisfactory."

As a military man Lee knew he could not win the war by remaining on the defensive; so in 1863 he led his troops into Northern territory. At the small town of Gettysburg in southern Pennsylvania, Lee's army met the Union forces in what proved to be the turning point of the Civil War. For three days (July 1-3) the two armies remained locked in a bloody battle. Finally, with forty per cent of his men killed or wounded, Lee retreated into Virginia.

Over the next two years Lee continued to pray that the Confederates would win the war. On several occasions he issued proclamations to the army setting aside days of fasting and prayer. He urged his men to humble themselves before God, confess their sins, and implore His mercy; however, as he had from the beginning, Lee left the Southern cause in God's hands. "We must," he said, "submit to His almighty will, whatever that may be."

Early in 1865 Lee became the chief commander of all Confederate forces, but by that time the Southern cause had already become hopeless. Realizing that further resistance would needlessly sacrifice the lives of his soldiers, Lee surrendered to General Ulysses S. Grant at Appomattox Court House, Virginia, on April 9, 1865. After signing the surrender document, Lee rode back to his troops and simply said, "Men, we have fought through the war together. I have done my best for you; my heart is too full to say more." Although the war officially came to an end soon after Lee's surrender, many people in both the North and South harbored a spirit of bitterness and hatred. Lee, however, did not succumb to such a divisive spirit but rather maintained a strong Christian testimony even in defeat. He said, "I have fought against the people of the North because I believed they were seeking to wrest from the South dearest rights. But I have never cherished toward them bitter or vindictive feelings, and have never seen the day when I did not pray for them."

It was in this spirit that Robert E. Lee the civilian took on new responsibilities after forty years of military service. In 1865 he accepted the presidency of Washington College (known today as Washington and Lee University) in Lexington, Virginia, where he served until his death five years later. As president Lee worked to improve the school academically, but he realized that the students needed more than a high quality curriculum. "I shall fail in the leading object that brought me here," he said, "unless these young men all become real Christians."

Each day the students met for chapel at 7:45 A.M. (8:45 in winter), a service led by various pastors from the surrounding area. Although some of the speakers preached impressive sermons, Lee expressed his love for simple, practical ones that reached the heart. On Sundays when there were no chapel services, Lee urged the young men to attend one of the nearby churches.

During the few years that Lee served at Washington College, he received a flood of other job offers, all of which promised lucrative salaries. For example, one company in New York City offered him $50,000 a year if he would join their organization. Politely turning down each offer, Lee chose to remain at the college and invest his time in the lives of young men. Even when the trustees tried to raise his salary, Lee refused it, saying that he had enough money to meet his needs.

When Lee died in October of 1870, he left behind him a heritage of exemplary service to his country and to his God. Even before the Civil War thrust him into national prominence, Lee had established Christian principles in his life. In a letter to his oldest son, dated April 5, 1852, Lee expressed one of the greatest of these principles: "Duty, then, is the sublimest word in our language. Do your duty in all things. . . . You cannot do more; you should never wish to do less."

Suggestions for Further Reading

Douglas Southall Freeman. *Lee.* New York: Scribner's, 1961. [Abridged by Richard Harwell from Freeman's exhaustive four-volume biography, *R. E. Lee*]

J. Williams Jones. *Life and Letters of Robert Edward Lee.* 1906. Reprint. Harrisonburg, Va.: Sprinkle Publications, 1978. [Written by a chaplain who served under Lee; emphasizes Lee's Christian character]

The Modern Era

(1865 to the Present)

The end of the Civil War initiated a period of growth and progress in American Christianity. Evangelism flourished, particularly through the great citywide campaigns of D. L. Moody, Sam Jones, Billy Sunday, and other evangelists. Encouraged by leaders such as Moody and energized by American expansion overseas, a new push in foreign missions emerged, the greatest since the Second Great Awakening. Led by inspiring figures such as Englishman Hudson Taylor, Canadian Jonathan Goforth, and American Lottie Moon, the missions movement resulted in the establishing of missionary efforts all around the world—Asia, Africa, and Latin America.

Challenged by the rise of religious liberalism—commonly called "modernism"—and the advent of Darwinian evolution, orthodoxy responded by creating Bible colleges and institutes, Bible conferences, and other means of propagating the truth. In addition, reform movements such as prohibition appeared to be succeeding in improving moral life in America. Before World War I, even staunch conservatives began to speak of establishing permanent world peace and to wonder whether the Millennium was dawning.

The First World War crushed this optimism, however, and ushered in an age of controversy. Liberalism increasingly emerged as a full-blown threat to Christianity. Orthodox Christians vigorously resisted the inroads of liberalism. To check the growth of cold formalism within their denomination, many Methodists embraced what became known as the Holiness movement. These Holiness Christians claimed that the Methodists had forgotten the teaching of founder John Wesley, particularly the need for heart-felt conversion and an upright life. Their characteristic teaching was "entire sanctification," the belief that after conversion a Christian could have his old sinful nature subdued by the Holy Spirit through a special work of grace. Empowerment by this work of grace, Holiness Christians believed, aided Christians in their striving for a holy life.

The Holiness movement rocked Methodism; more than a few observers thought that it might succeed in capturing the denomination

117

through its revivals, camp meetings, schools, and publications. Eventually, though, the movement fell short of its goal. Some advocates of Holiness teaching, dismayed by the antipathy of the Methodist hierarchy, broke away and formed their own denominations, such as the Church of the Nazarene. Those who remained within found themselves an increasingly embattled minority. The movement was also hurt by the rise of a distinct extremist group from within its ranks, the Pentecostals, who practiced even more dramatic "spiritual gifts," such as speaking in tongues and divine healing.

Other denominations, notably the Baptists and the Presbyterians, experienced their own conservative-liberal battle, what is commonly known as the fundamentalist-modernist controversy. "Fundamentalists," taking their name from *The Fundamentals* (a series of publications of the 1910s dedicated to defending the essential doctrines of orthodox Christianity), proposed "to do battle royal for the fundamentals." In the 1920s conservatives and liberals clashed over control of the major denominations, their schools, and their publishing houses. Christians in the South, where modernism was less of a threat, focused more on keeping evolution out of the public schools. These efforts ended in apparent failure. The liberal factions maintained control of the denominations, and the antievolution crusade faltered as a result of bad publicity and meager results. The nadir of the crusade was the circus atmosphere which surrounded the Scopes "Monkey Trial" in Tennessee, the most publicized court case concerning the ban on evolution.

Fundamentalism did not die, however. Rather than resign themselves to defeat, fundamentalists fought back by founding their own colleges and seminaries, mission boards, and publishing houses. Although often ignored in the media, fundamentalists underwent a period of growth throughout the 1930s and 1940s. Unfortunately, the movement split in the 1950s. One faction, preferring the name "new evangelical" or sometimes simply "evangelical," sought the support of religious liberals in hopes of gaining greater public and scholarly acceptance. The other faction, keeping the name "fundamentalist," maintained a strict separation from and opposition to liberalism.

Other movements were roiling the religious waters of twentieth-century America. The ecumenical movement sought to unite all nominally Christian churches into one body, regardless of theological differences among them. Two major expressions of "ecumenism" were the founding of the World Council of Churches in 1948 and the National Council of Churches in 1951 in America. Pentecostalism, which had remained somewhat of a fringe movement for the first half of the century, emerged transformed as the "charismatic movement" in the 1950s and 1960s. Like the earlier Pentecostals, Charismatics practiced speaking in tongues and divine healing, but they also differed in several ways.

The Modern Era (1865 to the Present)

Many Charismatics ignored or downplayed earlier Pentecostal strictures against "worldliness" (gambling, drinking, etc.). Most distinctively, Charismatics did not break with their denominations to join Pentecostal bodies. Charismatic Baptists, Lutherans, Methodists, and even Catholics appeared on the scene. As this variety would indicate, Charismatics tended to slight Christian doctrine in favor of religious experience.

What does the future hold for American Christianity? Some Christians, seeing the signs of decline about them, fear that conditions can only grow worse—although they offer the hope that at the darkest hour Christ at His Second Coming will establish a reign of righteousness through His sovereign power. Others, admitting the chaos of modern society, still hold to the hope of revival through a visitation of the Holy Spirit to restore the churches of America to spiritual life. Both views recognize, at any rate, that "every good and every perfect gift is from above, and cometh down from the Father of lights" (James 1:17). Only from God will salvation come.

Suggestions for Further Reading

David O. Beale. *In Pursuit of Purity: American Fundamentalism Since 1850*. Greenville, S.C.: Unusual Publications, 1986. [Probably the best narrative history of fundamentalism]

George Marsden. *Fundamentalism and American Culture*. New York: Oxford University Press, 1980. [Probably the best interpretive history of fundamentalism]

———. *Reforming Fundamentalism: Fuller Seminary and the New Evangelicalism*. Grand Rapids: Eerdmans, 1987. [The definitive study on the evangelical-fundamentalist split]

———. *Understanding Fundamentalism and Evangelicalism*. Grand Rapids: Eerdmans, 1991.

Ronald H. Nash. *Evangelicals in America*. Nashville: Abingdon, 1987.

Edward M. Panosian. *The World Council of Churches*. Greenville, S.C.: Bob Jones University Press, 1983. [A critique of the WCC from the fundamentalist perspective]

Timothy L. Smith. *Called Unto Holiness: The Story of the Nazarenes*. Kansas City, Mo.: Nazarene Publishing House, 1962. [The first three chapters (pp. 11-73) survey the background and early history of the Holiness movement.]

O. Talmadge Spence. *Pentecostalism: Purity or Peril?* Greenville, S.C.: Unusual Publications, 1989. [A history of Pentecostalism from a conservative perspective]

Vinson Synan. *The Holiness-Pentecostal Movement in the United States*. Grand Rapids: Eerdmans, 1971. [A survey from an avowedly pro-Charismatic perspective]

Moody and Sankey

by Bob Jones

*The growth of cities in the latter half of the nineteenth century
presented new challenges to the Church. These large urban
centers—with their teeming, anonymous masses—seemed to present a formidable obstacle to presenting the gospel to the lost. One
major Christian response was the development of "urban evangelism," the holding of great citywide meetings under the direction of
a leading evangelist. The pioneer of urban evangelism and possibly
its greatest exponent was Dwight L. Moody. "Water runs down
hill," Moody said, "and the highest hills in America are the great
cities. If we can stir them we shall stir the whole country."*

First in importance and in prominence among nineteenth-century
evangelists was Dwight Lyman Moody. Moody was born in Northfield,
Massachusetts, February 5, 1837. His mother being left a widow, he
was unable to attend school longer than a few months, and at the age
of seventeen he went to Boston and became a clerk in a shoe store. He
might have made a fortune in the shoe business, but he chose another
field. One writer, Grover C. Loud, states:

> The turning point in his life was simple, swift and direct. He
> was wrapping up a package of shoes. His Sunday School teacher
> at the Mount Vernon Street Congregational Church, Edward Kim-
> ball, dropped in on him and in a few earnest words urged him to
> give his allegiance to Jesus Christ. Moody paused, the string taut
> in his fingers. "I will," he replied . . . and for forty-five years,
> from that day in 1856 to his death on December 22, 1899, he
> never swerved from that pledge of fidelity.

Soon after his conversion Moody moved to Chicago, where he joined
the church and wanted to become a preacher. The deacons, however,
were not impressed with his efforts. The exuberant youth accepted their

decision, determined that he would then bring people to hear somebody else preach. He rented four pews and filled them each Sunday. He also recruited a Sunday school class of urchins which he taught himself.

Here Moody was swept into the Prayer Meeting Revival of 1857, the first revival he had encountered. He was filled with great zeal and corralled hundreds of members for a Sunday school that he organized among the slums of North Chicago. Fifteen hundred members outgrew North Market Hall; so Moody built a church for them. His avocation of soulwinning left little time for his vocation of shoe selling; so in 1860 he gave up business and devoted himself to city missionary work and, during the Civil War, to labors among the soldiers. He was active in the work of the YMCA and served as its president in Chicago from 1865 to 1869.

About this time Moody discovered that he could preach. He had taken the place of a scheduled speaker who failed to appear, and sixty conversions were the fruits of his first sermon. From that moment he dedicated his efforts to evangelism.

At the international convention of the YMCA at Indianapolis in 1870, Moody met Ira D. Sankey, who became his singer and lifelong partner in the evangelistic field. Sankey was a man of great personal charm and possessed a beautiful voice. Moody insisted from the moment he met him that Sankey join him as singer and music leader. This Sankey determined to do; and after returning to his home in New Castle, Pennsylvania, to arrange his affairs, he dedicated his life to the service of God in song. Throughout their whole ministry they were associated inseparably in the public mind. One spoke, not of meeting Moody, but rather of Moody and Sankey. During their first two years together, they were little known beyond the region around Chicago. Then they discovered England for evangelistic efforts, and England discovered them for America. From the summer of 1873 to the spring of 1875, they engaged in a series of meetings that shook that conservative nation as nothing had done since the time of Whitefield and the Wesleys.

When Moody returned to America in July 1875, he was the outstanding evangelist of the world. So wonderful was the work he had done in England that before he set sail for home he had received cables from half a dozen American cities beseeching his immediate presence for revival work. Moody decided on Brooklyn, New York, as the scene of his first effort in America. He and Sankey began their campaign on October 24, 1875, and remained there until November 19. Moody probably never worked harder than during those four weeks in Brooklyn. The results of this campaign, however, seem to have left him unsatisfied. Many professed conversion, and certainly the effects on the churches were good; yet in comparison with the meetings in Great Britain, this one left much to be desired. Moody felt that it was due to the shortness of time, and from then on he generally refused to accept engagements for brief campaigns.

Moody and Sankey moved on to Philadelphia where they conducted services in an abandoned railway depot which had been bought for a warehouse by businessman John Wanamaker. Wanamaker turned the building over to them after fitting it with seats. Here they remained until January 16. The total attendance during the two months was estimated at seven hundred thousand and the number of converts at four thousand. The following article on the Philadelphia campaign by George H. Stuart appeared in the *New York Tribune* on January 14, 1876:

> The last service of the eighth week of Moody and Sankey's labors in this city was attended this evening by over thirteen thousand persons, filling the great depot building to its utmost capacity. Many thousands were turned away, unable to obtain even standing room. The interest in these services has from the first steadily increased, and the labors of the evangelists have been and continue to be the all absorbing topics of conversation.

From Philadelphia Moody and Sankey journeyed to New York, where a campaign was begun February 7. On opening night twenty thousand people attempted to gain entrance to the Hippodrome where the services were held. The press reports of the campaign were glowing with praise of the evangelist. Moody, like all successful modern evangelists, knew how to use newspapers effectively, and up until his death was excellent "copy."

The *New York Daily Graphic,* in an editorial of April 25, said:

> The series of religious meetings held at the Hippodrome by Messrs. Moody and Sankey was in many respects the most remarkable ever held in this country. The meetings were a marked improvement on all previous great revivals in important particulars. They were well managed. The order was perfect. There was no disturbance, no rowdyism, no flippant jeering, no noisy vociferation of useless and inopportune amens. . . . The preaching was unlike that of previous revivalists in the fact that it was not exciting; it awoke no feelings of terror; it produced no spasms and agonies and convulsions; it sent nobody to the madhouse. It was pervaded with an undertone of sympathy and hope and love. . . . Whatever may be thought of Mr. Moody's doctrines, it must be conceded that he made a new departure revivalism.

After a summer's rest at Northfield, contrary to his stated purpose Moody held a series of brief campaigns in Nashville, Louisville, St. Louis, and Kansas City. The evangelist then began a crusade in Chicago, the seat of his early revival efforts. A large tabernacle had been built, and it was filled throughout the course of the revival with an eager, hungry throng. Here, as in other metropolitan centers, and perhaps even to a greater degree than in any, the revival commanded the attention of the dailies, and at the close of the campaign they received his public thanks.

Moody, like most great evangelists who preceded him, and like many of his prominent successors, never published an account of the number professing conversion. The only numerical results that can be accurately noted in any of his revivals are the number who joined churches. So it was in his Chicago campaign, at the close of which the *Tribune* stated:

> Mr. Moody has for a long time refused to give the number of hopeful conversions resulting from his meetings but the following facts and figures may serve to show the magnitude of the success of which over 10,000 or 12,000 of the Christians of Chicago and vicinity met to rejoice last evening. . . . The number of persons already received into the Chicago churches are set down as follows: Baptist 300; Congregational 300; Methodist 700; Presbyterian 750; besides many received into the German, Welsh, and other smaller churches not reported. It is safe to say that about 2500 new members have already been received into the churches of Chicago and vicinity, with perhaps an equal number known to the pastors who are expected to join at some future time.

In sharp contrast to the compromising modern ecumenical evangelism of Dr. Billy Graham, who welcomes modernistic and apostate pastors to his sponsoring committee, Moody was criticized for not doing so. The outstanding example of this was an open letter from the Rev. W. H. Ryder, pastor of St. Paul's Universalists Church. In this, the revivalist was taken to task in the *Tribune* of January 14, 1877, for allowing only "so-called evangelistic" churches to cooperate in the campaign, for his "persistent effort to show the worthlessness of morality as an element in the soul's salvation," and for the narrowness of his theology. Moody was not in the least disturbed, and the campaign was apparently helped by the opposition to it.

Several things occurred to throw a gloom over this series of meetings; yet, in spite of them all, Moody and Sankey considered them of great spiritual success. The first incident was the death of Moody's brother, necessitating his absence for a week to be with his aged mother. The second tragedy was the death of P. P. Bliss and his wife in a railroad wreck at Ashtabula, Ohio, as they were on their way to Chicago to assist in the campaign.

Bliss, a personal friend of both Moody and Sankey, was a hymn writer of great prominence and popularity. The tragic death of "the

Sweet Singer'' threw a pall over both the revivalists and their congregations. Services in his memory were held in the tabernacle and $10,000 raised for the two young Bliss children.

Despite opposition, criticism, and tragedy, the meetings were conceded to be most successful and were continued for some time after Moody and Sankey left by D. W. Whittle and George C. Stebbins, who worked with Moody in the evangelistic field.

Moody and Sankey next attacked the center of New England Unitarianism and conservatism. They began their efforts in Boston on January 28, 1877. For both the afternoon and evening of the initial day, the doors were opened long before the time announced, and the building was at once filled, and overflow services were held in other halls. The press did not hail Moody as warmly as it had in other places, and the *Boston Transcript* said, ''It was the remark of many that in Moody they were disappointed and in Mr. Sankey they were surprised.'' Moody's voice was described as ''unpleasant'' and his manner as ''abrupt,'' but it was conceded that he was ''brief'' and ''forceful.''

It was not long, however, until populace, press, and Protestant preachers were nearly unanimous in supporting the campaign. Phillips Brooks, pastor of the prestigious Trinity Episcopal Church, was active from the beginning. It was he who pronounced the benediction on the first evening of the revival; and on another occasion when Moody was absent, he preached for him in the tabernacle. Moody and Sankey were tireless in their efforts. There are records of as many as four services in one day, the last being a prayer meeting following the evening service, for which two thousand persons remained.

Conservative New England was being thoroughly awakened. Railroads offered half-fare excursion rates from nearby towns to persons desiring to attend the campaign. ''The seventh week of the revival effort continued with no apparent diminution of interest'' according to the March 12 *Transcript*. The tabernacle was crowded and hundreds were turned away from three services a day.

On Monday, May 21, just before the close of the campaign, Moody addressed the ministers who had cooperated in the series of meetings. He urged them to provide a warm church home for the new converts and stressed the necessity of feeding the flock. The ministers attempted to persuade Moody to remain another year and continue his efforts of evangelizing New England. They ''had noticed a remarkable change here and at Harvard College'' and ''were pleased to note the decline of the literary indifference which had been so common,'' according to the May 22 *Transcript*. Moody's Boston campaign was followed up by L. W. Munhall, an evangelist of great power and spirituality.

The season of 1877-78 was also spent by Moody and Sankey in New England—this time in visiting a number of leading cities. According to

Faith of Our Fathers: Scenes from American Church History

Frank Beardsley's *History of American Revivals,* "Thousands were converted and all New England felt the impulse of the revivals with which these cities had been visited."

During 1878-79 meetings were held in Baltimore, in which all the evangelical denominations of the city cooperated. These services closed on May 26 after nearly eight months of duration, during a large part of which another campaign was being conducted only a few blocks away by Thomas Harrison. The meetings did not interfere with each other, however, and Beardsley said, "Baltimore was greatly blessed in this double visitation."

Moody, during the remainder of the nineteenth century, continued to draw great crowds and have splendid results in revival meetings throughout the U.S. The most outstanding single effort was his campaign in Chicago during the period of the Columbian Exposition. Moody divided the city into districts, in each of which services were held by assisting evangelists and the students of the Bible Institute which he had founded on the North Side. Moody himself preached to great throngs that crowded a tent on the Midway each Sunday to hear the gospel proclaimed amidst the babble of the carnival.

This Chicago campaign may be considered the climax of Moody's spectacular career. Though he continued to preach up until a few days before his death, his powers were visibly on the wane. His death on December 22, 1899, was symbolic of the passing of the century of great evangelists, of whom none left a more indelible imprint than Dwight Lyman Moody.

Moody was always a disciple of love. His sermons stressed the divine love, and that has been suggested as the key to his great success. Moody was not a great scholar, nor essentially a great preacher. One of his biographers, W. R. Moody, said, "The sermon that could hold the rapt attention of the most intelligent of his congregation would also be listened to with the same eagerness by the children present." His faith was that of a child. Practical and sensible, Moody was never given to extreme positions on doctrine and was kindly but intolerant of evil. He considered himself simply a preacher who had a definite duty to God and man. Gamaliel Bradford sums up the ministry of Dwight L. Moody in these well-chosen words: "In his day, none worked more passionately, more lovingly, and more successfully to bring God to man and man to God."

Suggestions for Further Reading
James F. Findlay. *Dwight L. Moody: American Evangelist, 1837-1899.*
Chicago: University of Chicago Press, 1969. [Probably the best scholarly biography of Moody]

Keith J. Hardman. *The Spiritual Awakeners.* Chicago: Moody Press, 1983. [See pp. 189-208.]

W. R. Moody. *The Life of Dwight L. Moody.* 1900. Reprint. Murfreesboro, Tenn.: Sword of the Lord Publishers, n.d. [Written by Moody's son]

John C. Pollock. *Moody: A Biographical Portrait.* New York: Macmillan, 1963.

"The Unconventional Dwight L. Moody." *Christian History,* vol. 9, no. 1 (1990). [Entire issue]

Fanny Crosby: The Blind Poetess

by Carolyn P. Cooper

The late nineteenth century was the golden age of the "gospel song," sacred tunes less formal than hymns with popular, easily sung melodies. Numerous composers and hymn writers contributed to the genre; Ira Sankey, P. P. Bliss, Frances Ridley Havergal, and E. O. Excell are just a few. The evangelistic campaigns of Moody and Sankey in particular served to popularize the gospel song, and they popularized no songs more than those of Fanny Crosby, who was perhaps the greatest of all the gospel songwriters.

"What will you do without me? You have never been away from home more than two weeks of your life." Fanny's determination wavered for a moment, but as soon as she remembered that the desire of her heart was about to be fulfilled, she said, "Much as I love you, Mother, I am willing to make any sacrifice to acquire an education."

With this adamant decision, the small blind girl was helped into the carriage that would carry her away from home and all that was familiar to a new, unknown world. This same determination was evident throughout her life and contributed in making Fanny Crosby, called by many "the queen of sacred songs," one of the most outstanding hymn writers that the world has ever known.

Born on March 24, 1820, in Putnam County, New York, Frances Jane Crosby was the normal healthy child of John and Mercy Crosby. Six months later, however, a new doctor in the community was called in to treat an inflammation of their first-born daughter's eyes. His remedy, applying hot poultices to the child's eyes, caused permanent damage. Fanny Crosby was blinded.

Being blind, however, did not stop Fanny from enjoying her childhood. She learned to sing, play the guitar, climb a tree, and ride a galloping horse while clinging tightly to its mane. Her favorite times, however, were spent with her grandmother. This godly woman delighted in teaching her granddaughter about the beauties of nature and the wonders found in the Holy Scriptures. From her grandmother, Fanny learned the names and descriptions of dozens of birds, trees, and flowers. She came to love the violet, and it remained her favorite flower throughout her life. It was also through her grandmother's influence that the Bible became Fanny's favorite book. "It was Grandma who brought the Bible to me, and me to the Bible," Fanny later recalled. Before the age of fifteen, she was able to repeat the entire Pentateuch, the Gospels, most of the Psalms, Proverbs, Ruth, and selections from the Prophets. It was from this abundant storehouse that she would later draw her heart-warming hymns.

Her natural poetic ability became evident at an early age. When only eight years old, Fanny wrote this poem:

O what a happy soul am I!
Although I cannot see,
I am resolved that in this world
Contented I will be.

How many blessings I enjoy,
That other people don't.
To weep and sigh because I'm blind,
I cannot, and I won't.

She had accepted her blindness at this early age, but she had not accepted the limitations placed upon the blind. Fanny's quest for knowledge was never ending. She desired more than anything to attend school, but in those days schooling for the blind was not widespread. Fanny often prayed, "Dear Lord please show me how I can learn like other children." But it was not until 1834, when she was fourteen, that her mother heard about the New York Institution for the Blind. It was immediately decided that Fanny would go there to study, a decision that became a turning point in the young girl's life.

"Victorious living" could have been the motto of the Institution. "We were taught that whatever we determined to do, if within the average power of man or woman we could, with God's help, do the same as if we had the blessings of sight: and at it we went with a will." Fanny Crosby determined to do many things with her life. She excelled in grammar, philosophy, astronomy, and political economy. She learned how to play the piano, the organ, and the harp. She had a remarkable memory; someone had only to read a book aloud to her one time and the contents were indelibly stamped upon her mind. She could recall bits of verses and articles from newspapers for years after she had heard them. She could write a poem about almost anything. She was often asked to write poetry for special occasions: birthdays, funerals, weddings, anniversaries, and even national events. Her teachers and classmates lauded her with praises. Fanny was the prize pupil at the Institution. Her first book, *A Blind Girl and Other Poems,* was published in 1844.

During her twenty-three years at the Institution, both as a student and as a teacher, Fanny was called upon to entertain many people. Some noteworthy visitors who also became Fanny's friends were President James K. Polk, Henry Clay, and General Winfield Scott. For all of these men she wrote and recited special poems, and they did not forget the blind woman who had graciously entertained them. Fanny also often traveled across the country on public relations missions for the Institution for the Blind. In an appeal for aid in educating the blind, she was even called upon to recite her poetry before the U.S. Congress. The petite young woman with long black curls and dark rectangular spectacles drew attention wherever she went. Fanny Crosby's fame as "the Blind Poetess" spread.

During the spring of 1849, cholera killed thousands in New York City. While many fled to the country to escape death, Fanny volunteered to stay behind and work as a nurse. For months, she diligently cared for victims of the raging pestilence. As she sat beside the bedside of a dying patient, listening to the cry of the undertaker in the street—"Bring out your dead!"—her heartbeat quickened. "I'm not prepared to die," she thought. Although she had been tutored by a godly Christian grandmother and had committed much of the Bible to memory, Fanny was not at peace. At her grandmother's deathbed, Fanny had promised to meet her in heaven, but she had never really considered what it meant to face death. She was greatly troubled, realizing that she was not prepared to die.

A close friend and colleague, Theodore Camp, invited the questing Fanny to a revival meeting in the Broadway Tabernacle. On November 20, 1850, during the last verse of Isaac Watts's "Alas and Did My Saviour Bleed?" Fanny gave herself completely to God. It is significant that one of the greatest hymn writers in the world came to Christ through the words of a hymn.

Fanny now waited to see how God would use her in His service. She continued to teach rhetoric, grammar, and Roman and American history at the Institution. She continued to entertain people, such as the famous opera star Jenny Lind and future president Grover Cleveland, with her poetry. And she continued to write. But desiring to do more with her life, she waited for guidance.

It was during this interim that Fanny and another blind teacher at the Institution fell in love. Alexander Van Alstyne, a talented musician, had come to the Institution five years after Fanny. They married in 1858 and left their teaching positions. Not much is recorded of the Van Alstynes' life together, but they were known as a generous-hearted couple who often taught classical music to poor children who lived around them. Alexander also was a paid organist for several local churches in New York. He occasionally supplied music for some of Fanny's poems. The death of their newborn baby in 1859 caused Fanny to plunge herself even deeper into her writing.

With her love for God and her love for poetry, Fanny's call to service soon became evident. In 1863 she met the noted musician William B. Bradbury. He had heard of Mrs. Van Alstyne's poetry and greeted her by saying, "Fanny, I thank God that we have met at last, for I think you can write hymns." With encouragement, she published her first hymn in 1864, "We Are Going, We Are Going." This was the beginning of a fifty-one year career as a hymn writer. Fanny had finally found her mission. "I was the happiest creature in all the world," she declared. She produced thousands of hymns, many of which are favorites today. The extreme simplicity of her hymns appealed to the common people of her day. She wrote hymns to reach the hearts of the poor, the destitute, and the sinful: "Rescue the Perishing," "Jesus Is Tenderly Calling," "Saved By Grace," and "Blessed Assurance." One biographer wrote that "it was her power to speak the language of the people which has made the world take Fanny Crosby to its heart."

Because she had become known to the public as Fanny Crosby, the Blind Poetess, she published under that name even after her marriage. But her writing became so prolific that she often used pen names so that her publishers' hymnals would not be filled with songs written *only* by Fanny Crosby. Some of these names were derivatives of Fanny's own name, and others were those of favorite friends or relatives. She signed many of her hymns "Fannie," "F.A.N.," "Mrs. Van A.," "Ella Dale," "Mrs. E. A. Andrews," "Victoria Francis," and "Julia Stirling." In all, Fanny used 204 different pen names!

It is amazing that one person could produce so much in her lifetime. Fanny became so adept at writing poetry that she was often called upon to supply the words to a tune on short notice. This was the case in one of her most famous hymns, "Safe in the Arms of Jesus." Dr. William H. Doane, who had been composing tunes for Fanny's poetry, stopped one day at the Van Alstyne house while on his way to Cincinnati. He played a tune on the piano for Fanny, leaving her forty minutes to write the words before his train left. She said that the tune sounded like "Safe in the Arms of Jesus," and she had the hymn written for him within thirty minutes.

In her own life story, Fanny told how she was often inspired to write:

There were some days, or at least hours, when I could not compose a hymn if the world were laid at my feet as a promised recompense. So what would I do if it were necessary or highly desirable that a hymn be written on a certain day or night? If I were not in the mood to write, I would build a mood—or, try to draw one around me. I should sit alone, as I have done many a day and a night, praying God to give me the thoughts and the feelings wherewith to compose a hymn. After a time—perhaps not unmingled with struggle—the ideas would come, and I would soon be happy in my verse.

God had called Fanny Crosby to a specific job for a specific time. Her indirect influence in the great revival meetings of D. L. Moody and Ira D. Sankey cannot be measured. They were responsible for the spread and popularity of Fanny's hymns across the ocean. Sankey's singing of his favorite of Fanny's hymns, "Pass Me Not, O Gentle Saviour," drew thousands of repentant sinners to the altar. Sankey, whose own eyesight failed in later life, was described by Fanny as "a never-failing friend." He called Fanny to his bedside before he died, asking her if she got to heaven before him to watch for him at the pearly gate at the eastern side of the "city four square." He said, "When I get there, I will take you by the hand and lead you along the Golden Street to the Throne of God, and there we will stand before the Lamb and say:

And now we see Thee face to face,
Saved by Thy matchless, boundless grace,
And we are satisfied."

But Fanny did not precede Sankey to heaven. She had many more years of service before she saw her Lord's face. Though a small, delicate woman, Fanny had boundless energy. Even in her old age, she could tire out people twenty and thirty years her junior. Besides producing a profusion of hymns, Fanny also was active in speaking engagements. Her talks, like her hymns, were simple, direct, and personal. After she was sixty, she considered her chief occupation that of home mission worker. Many of her hymns were written expressly for use in the New York missions where she worked. She was also a regular lecturer at the railroad branch of the YMCA. Fanny delighted in calling the railroad men "my boys," and it is estimated that over the years she "adopted" nearly six hundred of them. It was at this time that she began to be lovingly addressed as "Aunt Fanny."

Even as she grew older, Fanny found little time to rest. Resting was for old people, she said, and she was young. She felt that as long as she kept busy, she would always be young. Hymn writing still continued to be her greatest joy. She claimed, "It is my life's work and I cannot tell you what pleasure I derive from it. I believe I would not live a year if my work were taken from me." Her door was continually open to visitors who flocked to "Aunt Fanny" for advice on all subjects. She was never too busy to receive anybody who came to see her. Though she might be anticipating a twelve- or fourteen-hour day crammed with lectures, mission work, and writing, she always interrupted what she was doing to spend time with her callers. She loved people, and it was evident that they loved her.

Fanny outlived her husband, who died in 1902, and most of her friends and relatives. Although blind, she never considered herself handicapped. She lived a long, full life of service, until on February 12, 1915, at the age of ninety-four, the Blind Poetess finally met her Saviour face to face. She left behind a rich heritage of sacred songs that have touched the hearts of saints and sinners alike. Shortly after her death, it was estimated that more than a hundred million copies of her eight thousand hymns had been published. Many of them have been translated into foreign languages, and today wherever the gospel is preached, the songs of Fanny Crosby are sung.

Suggestions for Further Reading

Fanny J. Crosby. *An Autobiography.* 1906. Reprint. Grand Rapids: Baker, 1986.

Guye Johnson. *Treasury of Great Hymns and Their Stories.* Greenville, S.C.: Bob Jones University Press, 1986. [Describes the circumstances behind the writing of ''Pass Me Not, O Gentle Saviour,'' ''All the Way My Saviour Leads Me,'' and ''Blessed Assurance'' as well as ninety-seven hymns by other writers]

Benjamin Breckinridge Warfield and the Defense of the Scriptures

by Mark Sidwell

In the nineteenth century the Christian faith withstood numerous assaults. Evolutionists, following the course set down by Charles Darwin in his Origin of Species, *attacked the historical and scientific veracity of the book of Genesis. Even more surprisingly, supposed "Christian theologians" advanced theories on the nature and origin of the Scriptures that cast doubt on and even denied their supernatural character. Not all theologians were so unbelieving in their approach to the Bible, however. In America none were more zealous and firm in their defense of orthodox Christianity than the theologians of Princeton Theological Seminary. And no Princeton theologian was greater in his learning, clarity of expression, and fidelity to God's Word than B. B. Warfield, who affirmed plainly, "The Scriptures are throughout a Divine book, created by the Divine energy and speaking in every part with Divine authority directly to the heart of the readers."*

"If we wish to put a proper estimate upon Dr. Warfield's work," said Francis L. Patton, former president of Princeton Seminary, in 1921, "we must fully understand his theological position, and the key to that position is his unfaltering belief in the inspiration of the Old and New Testaments." In the nineteenth century there were few men more learned or more determined in their defense of the inspiration of the Scriptures than Benjamin B. Warfield. He was a man who could have easily borne the name of one of John Bunyan's characters in *Pilgrim's Progress,* "Valiant-for-Truth."

An intensely private and reserved man, Warfield left few records or reminiscences that shed light on his personal life. We know that he was born near Lexington, Kentucky, in 1851, and that he made his first public profession of his faith in Christ when he joined the Presbyterian church at the age of sixteen. He made an excellent record at Princeton College, graduating with highest honors in 1871. Warfield showed particular aptitude for and deep interest in science and mathematics, but he surprised—without displeasing—his family when he announced suddenly that he was going to prepare for the ministry. Although he graduated from Princeton Theological Seminary in 1876 and held two pastorates, Warfield made his greatest mark not in the pulpit but in the classroom. He served as a professor at Western Theological Seminary in Pittsburgh, and in 1887 he came to Princeton, where he enjoyed a rich ministry for the rest of his life.

Founded in 1812 as a citadel for orthodox Christianity, Princeton Theological Seminary suited Warfield well. For over thirty years he served at the seminary, using his position there to expound and to defend the Christian faith. Part of Warfield's impact for orthodoxy was felt by his students in the classroom. He possessed a distinguished, gentlemanly presence that lent solemn weight to his words. "There was something remarkable in his voice," fellow professor Francis L. Patton said. "It had the liquid softness of the South. . . . His words proceeded out of his mouth as if they walked on velvet." A man of keen intellect, Warfield did not hesitate to cross swords with students who challenged him on points of doctrine. "Sometimes he would use the Socratic method on a reciter," one student recalled, "and lead some student disposed to argue into a series of statements which drove the young liberal into the orthodox corner where 'Benny' wanted him." Warfield also used humor and illustration to drive home his point. A former student described one such incident in full:

> Once someone asked the difference between predestination and fatalism. In answer Dr. Warfield told a story of a small boy in Holland who went too near the long revolving arms of his father's windmill. The father cautioned the lad to keep away from the windmill, lest some day his clothes be caught on the revolving arms and he be dashed to pieces. For a while the boy obeyed, but one day he forgot or just ignored his father's warning, and went near the mill. After a while suddenly he felt himself jerked up by the clothing and heavily thumped again and again with great force on the seat of his baggy Dutch trousers. His first thought was: "Oh, I am being pounded to pieces, the windmill has caught me!" Then he looked around and saw the angry face of his father over him and realized he was receiving a good old-fashioned Dutch spanking administered by his angry parent.
>
> "Now," said Dr. Warfield, "if he had been really in the arms of the windmill, that would have been like fatalism, man in the grip of a machine. But in predestination we are in the hands of a Heavenly Father—but the spanking feels just as hard."

Warfield had no time for the idea that it is somehow more "spiritual" to be unlearned and that it is somehow a mark of piety to refuse to study. "Why should you turn from God when you turn to your books, or feel that you must turn from your books in order to turn to God?" he asked. When faced with the facile argument that "ten minutes on your knees will give you a truer, deeper, more operative knowledge of God than ten hours over your books," he replied, why not "ten hours over your books on your knees"? Education was vitally important for the minister, thought Warfield, but he did not neglect piety. "A minister must be learned, on pain of being utterly incompetent for his work. But before and above being learned, a minister must be godly."

As important as Warfield's classroom ministry was, it is his writing that is remembered today. Some of the professors at Princeton wrote large, single works of theology. For instance, Charles Hodge (1797-1878), one of Warfield's teachers and predecessors, wrote a three-volume *Systematic Theology* that is commonly considered the finest comprehensive expression of the theology of the Princeton position. Although Warfield wrote some such books, he lent most of his efforts to writing numerous articles and essays in which he brilliantly and unflinchingly refuted the false teachings of his day. It was in these articles that Warfield gave fullest expression to his views and left his richest legacy to the Church. The editor of a series of Warfield's writings wrote, "What most impresses the student of Warfield's writings—apart from his deeply religious spirit, his sense of complete dependence on God for all things including especially his sense of indebtedness as a lost sinner to His free grace—is the breadth of his learning and the exactness of his scholarship."

Warfield gained his greatest fame, perhaps, for his defense of the orthodox doctrine of the inspiration of Scripture. In his day, liberal theologians in Europe and increasingly in America had begun to apply the idea of evolution rationalistically to the Bible in a manner that destroyed its divine authority. For example, these "higher critics," as they came to be known, denied that Moses had written the Pentateuch and asserted that most of the Old Testament was the product of a literary evolution involving centuries of work by priests and scribes in blending the myths, legends, and perhaps a little genuine history of the Hebrew people into the books we know today. Warfield refuted them on two grounds. First, he wrote scholarly historical treatises pointing out the flaws in research and reasoning that had led the critics astray into their erroneous conclusions.

Second, he fully and systematically expounded the Scripture's teaching concerning its own inspiration and authority. With Princeton professor A. A. Hodge, he wrote a treatise, *Inspiration* (1881), that plainly asserted and defended the proposition that the Bible is the infallible

Word of God, completely without error and entirely trustworthy in authority. In another article in 1915, Warfield gave a simple yet classic and profound definition of the doctrine: "Inspiration is . . . a supernatural influence exerted on the sacred writers by the Spirit of God, by virtue of which their writings are given Divine trustworthiness." In a memorial address, Francis L. Patton said of Warfield's defense of inspiration, "In this he was rendering a great service to multitudes of faithful ministers who for lack of adequate learning were themselves unable to vindicate their faith in the Word of God. His fearless belief was a buttress to men as he stood foresquare [sic] to every wind that blows in his unshaken confidence in the oracles of God."

Warfield became ill on Christmas Eve, 1920, recovered briefly, and then died on February 16, 1921. Regrettably, within a few years after his death, Princeton Theological Seminary began turning from the orthodox Christianity he taught and defended to the liberal infidelity he opposed. But Princeton's apostasy could not undo the benefit he had already given to the Church. One of his students, over twenty years after Warfield's death, wrote in memorial: "But his memory is blessed and his influence is still potent in the life and convictions of those who gathered before him in old Stuart Hall; and the Princeton Theology of Paul and Augustine and Calvin and the Alexanders and the Hodges and Patton and Warfield is ever and again most irritatingly alive and dynamic just when its enemies think they have given it the deathstroke."

Suggestions for Further Reading

A. A. Hodge and Benjamin B. Warfield. *Inspiration.* 1881. Reprint. Grand Rapids: Baker, 1979. [The classic presentation of Warfield's defense of the doctrine]

Samuel G. Craig. "Benjamin B. Warfield." Introduction to *Biblical and Theological Studies,* by Benjamin B. Warfield, pp. xi-xlvii. Philadelphia: Presbyterian and Reformed, 1968.

W. Andrew Hoffecker. *Piety and the Princeton Theologians.* Phillipsburg, N.J.: Presbyterian and Reformed, 1981. [See pp. 95-155.]

Mark A. Noll, ed. *The Princeton Theology, 1812-1921.* Phillipsburg, N.J.: Presbyterian and Reformed, 1983. [See the introduction (pp. 11-48) and pp. 239-319.]

Sam Jones, Great Evangelist

by Bob Jones

Between D. L. Moody and Billy Sunday stand a host of other evangelists, not as famous, perhaps, but no less instrumental in the winning of the lost to Christ through great citywide meetings. R. A. Torrey, J. Wilbur Chapman, Bob Jones, Sr., William Biederwolf, and "Gipsy" Smith are but a few. One of the greatest of these men was the preacher often called "the Moody of the South," Evangelist Sam Jones.

Sam Jones of Cartersville, Georgia, was an eccentric, small-town lawyer, a member of the bar but given to drink and apparently uninterested in spiritual matters. In 1872 Sam Jones's father died. By his father's deathbed Sam promised to quit drinking. A few weeks later Sam was converted in a revival being held by his grandfather. From that day he was a changed man. He had always been a person of ready wit and humor, but drink had reduced him to a dissipated drayman. Yet after his conversion, he became the most striking evangelist that America has ever known.

Three months after his conversion, he was admitted to the North Georgia Conference of the Methodist Episcopal Church South, in those days committed to the authority and inspiration of Scripture, and was assigned to a circuit of five congregations. For eight years Sam Jones labored in the itinerancy, but in 1880, at his request, he was appointed agent of the North Georgia Orphans Home. This appointment left much of his time free for evangelistic work. While yet a circuit rider, he had held many revivals in towns with populations from 1,000 to 2,500 and had become greatly in demand for evangelistic work. Later he held meetings in many larger towns, including Atlanta, where he won some fame as a revivalist, and as a result was invited by the Protestant ministers of Memphis, Tennessee, to conduct a union revival campaign in that city.

The Memphis meeting was his first meeting outside his native state, but it brought Sam Jones to the attention of the entire South. "His next great meeting held at Nashville attracted the attention not only of the South but of the entire nation,'' noted Jones's wife after his death. Jones so won the hearts of the people of Nashville that they offered to buy him a home if he would take up his permanent residence in that city. He refused the offer with thanks, for he felt that he owed his first allegiance to his native state.

The *Christian Advocate,* the publication of Mr. Jones's own church, carried a four-page editorial on his Nashville campaign, from which the following is quoted:

> Sam Jones has the floor. His sayings and doings are the current subject of conversation, not only in Nashville, but all over the immense region of which it is the geographical and literary center. He is the man of the hour. His preaching in Nashville during the past two weeks has been attended by unprecedented crowds and with the most extraordinary results. Drunkards have renounced their liquor drinking; gamblers have given up their evil occupation; church members, convicted of complicity with sin, have broken off from wrong courses; thousands of persons of all ages, sexes and grades of society have publicly announced their purpose to give up their sins and live better lives.

Sam Jones held great meetings up and down America. Wherever he went, he drew large crowds and became the center of conversation. In St. Louis the *Globe-Democrat* and *Republic* covered his first meeting extensively. When he finished that campaign at the close of 1885, he was known throughout the territory.

Sam Jones began the year 1886 with an attack on the city which Moody himself called ''the graveyard for evangelists,'' Cincinnati. The meeting began rather slowly, but before it closed, the whole city was involved. While he was in Cincinnati, D. L. Moody stopped off the train one night to hear Jones preach and upon his return to the station wrote to congratulate Jones on his shattering attacks against the formalism of the church.

In Chicago, where he next preached, Mr. Jones found his fame had preceded him. The Reverend Sam Small of Atlanta, Mr. Jones's associate in evangelistic work, and almost as much of a character, had been holding advance services for some time, and he had set up an elaborate organization. Workers had been trained to serve as ushers at the converted skating rink where the services were to be held. A corps had been enlisted for house-to-house visitation in the interest of the revival. Dispatches from Georgia had preceded the evangelist, telling of his temperance activity and revival work. A reporter from a Chicago paper boarded the train on which Jones was riding while it was some miles from Chicago and interviewed him as they came into the city. The results of that interview occupied several columns in the Sunday edition.

Jones was asked if he would use any special tactics in dealing with the wickedness of Chicago. He replied that the sins were the same as in any other city and that his methods had been successful against them elsewhere. When the reporter called Jones's attention to criticism of Sam Small's slang, Jones replied, "Small is as chaste as Addison compared with me. If they can't stand him, they will be seized with vomiting when they hear me."

The meeting in Chicago was one of the most spectacular Jones ever held. The daily papers published his sermons in full from stenographic reportings. The evangelist received many letters commending him for his work, and the cooperating pastors were more than usually loyal to the evangelist and, at the close of the campaign, publicly expressed their appreciation to him for his efforts. Sam Jones won the approval of the Bible-believing, Christ-honoring, and gospel-preaching ministers who were at that time still in the majority in the churches of any city across America.

He did not hesitate to preach against theater-going, dancing, or card playing on the part of church members. He was incessant in his demand for a "strait-edge religion." Yet the more fiery his preaching, the greater the crowds that came to hear him.

Both Small and Jones were greatly criticized for their use of tobacco, a custom which was common among ministers of the South but which was looked upon as unclerical in the North. One of the outstanding Chicago pastors defended their use of tobacco in a sermon to his congregation, but both of the evangelists announced from the pulpit that they had given up tobacco smoking since they did not wish to do anything that would stand in a sinner's way. It is evident that this decision cost Jones some struggle, for he was several days slower than Small in making his decision.

On the closing night of the campaign, 10,000 people were turned away, and it was estimated that 260,000 people heard the evangelist during the course of the revival.

Among his subsequent campaigns, the one that Sam Jones held in Boston is noteworthy. This campaign under the auspices of the Methodist Union opened on January 16 with grave misgivings of many of Jones's friends who feared his slang and personal peculiarities might be distasteful to a New England audience. As usual, his friends were surprised. At the close of the meeting Sam Jones said, "Nowhere have I been criticized as little as I have been criticized in Boston. I want to say that nowhere have I preached the Gospel more plainly than I have preached it in Boston. Brethren, some people think that Sam Jones has modified by coming to Boston. I have been a little worse here than common."

In the Boston work, Jones was again assisted by Sam Small. The music was under the direction of E. O. Excell, who for many years was associated with the Georgia evangelist. Great crowds filled the churches in which the Southerners preached, with even greater crowds being turned away. To the people of the Pacific Coast in 1889, and throughout America, until the day of his death, Sam Jones carried the gospel. Always, he was just himself.

On October 15, 1906, as he was returning home from a meeting in Oklahoma City, he died aboard a train as it was standing on the track near Little Rock, Arkansas. His body was brought on a special train to Cartersville, where Bishop Charles B. Galloway gave the funeral oration. On the following day the body was taken to Atlanta where it lay in state in the rotunda of the Georgia capitol. Ministers and laymen alike mourned for one who, from riding a circuit in the hills of North Georgia, had become a beloved and outstanding national figure.

Suggestions for Further Reading

Clyde E. Fant and William M. Pinson, Jr. *20 Centuries of Great Preaching.* Vol. 6. *Spurgeon to Meyer, 1834-1929.* Waco, Texas: Word Books, 1971. [See pp. 321-63 for a ten-page biographical sketch of Jones and four of his sermons.]

Laura McElwain Jones. *The Life and Sayings of Sam P. Jones.* 1907. Reprint. St. John, Ind.: Christian Book Gallery, n.d. [Written by Jones's wife]

A. T. Pierson: Servant of God

by Christa G. Habegger

In the late nineteenth century, American churches were trum-peting great "forward movements" in Christianity: a new push in foreign missions, the creation of Bible conferences and Bible institutes, a fresh emphasis on the study of Bible prophecy, a resurgence of interest in the Biblical concept of holiness, and a surge in the publishing of Christian literature. A. T. Pierson, the man who coined the phrase "forward movements," actively par-ticipated in them all. If, as one historian suggests, the period from 1890 to 1917 was "The Era of Crusades," then A. T. Pierson was one of the chief crusaders.

The year 1837 introduced a significant era in world history. Young Queen Victoria ascended the throne of Great Britain. Interest in world exploration peaked and missionary societies flourished. Within a very few years, the telegraph would be in operation and the Atlantic Ocean made less formidable by the safe passage of *The Great Western.* On March 6, 1837, Martin Van Buren officially assumed the presidency of the United States. On the same day, Arthur Tappan Pierson was born to Stephen and Sally Ann Pierson of New York. He grew up—not to change the history of the world—but to influence thousands of lives for eternity.

The ninth child in a family of ten, Arthur Pierson enjoyed the blessings of a godly home. His parents resolved to rear their children to be Christian servants. Each child was taught the catechism and Scripture verses. Family devotions, held both morning and evening, helped to shield the youngster from worldly temptations outside the home. Young Arthur benefited greatly from his Sunday school attendance at church. There he was taught the doctrines of inspiration, regeneration, and the deity of Christ. There, too, he got his first introduction to foreign missions and began to envision himself as a preacher. Years later a biographer recorded that "one of Arthur's favorite pastimes was preaching to his sisters or to a row of empty chairs—the latter proving to be the more quiet audience."

From his childhood Arthur was a willing scholar with an insatiable desire for learning. His parents recognized the need for formal training and sacrificed to send him to private institutions where he was thoroughly grounded in classical literature, the sciences, and oratory. The Bible was a required textbook and the scholars were "encouraged to pray habitually and to live in the consciousness that there is a world beyond this." By age twelve Arthur was reading the New Testament in Greek. At thirteen he faced an important question: "Shall I seek great things for myself in my own way, or shall I give my life to God and surrender to the claims of Jesus Christ?" He made his decision to accept Christ at a church altar following a revival meeting. Arthur was serious about his conversion. On the way back to the school ward where he and his classmates boarded, he felt that he must be a good testimony before his unsaved companions. Arthur recalled, "As I undressed for bed, I asked God for courage and then . . . knelt down. . . and silently prayed. The boys . . . began to chuckle, and presently a pillow came flying at my head." When Arthur continued in prayer, "one of the older boys said, 'Let him alone,' and silently they all . . . got into bed." Arthur said that having won this first battle, "I was never again disturbed when praying before my fellows."

College training sharpened Arthur's already keen talents. He excelled particularly in writing essays and poems and in public speaking. Tall and slim with dark, wavy hair, large expressive eyes, and an intense, convincing manner, young Pierson used his natural gifts to good advantage. His classmates considered him the best speaker among them. Rather than devote himself solely to intellectual pursuits, as he might have done, Arthur centered much of his activity on church work and personal witnessing. In his diary he recorded many conversions—among them one of his college teachers.

Although Pierson's life was outwardly pure and his Christian service sincere and energetic, there was a time when "in the course of his scientific studies his inquiring mind became a little skeptical on some points which he had been taught to believe." Later he recorded this testimony of his battle with doubt: "Just as I was leaving college, I felt myself in danger of sinking into . . . doubt. I had been much interested in the study of the natural sciences and read many books on the subject, written by unbelievers. A shallow knowledge of science was leading me into skepticism, but I found that the deeper I went into the study, the more surely I came upon the reality of God. I found . . . that all true science leads to the divine Creator and ruler of the universe.

During college, Arthur had met Frances Benedict, the girl who would one day be his wife. Despite their attraction to each other, their wedding did not occur until four years later after Arthur completed seminary.

Arthur's bride-to-be was well educated, and her quiet and retiring nature would suit her for their lifelong ministry together.

During Arthur's three years of seminary study he did much to prove his "book" knowledge by practical application. He taught a church Bible class, visited prisons, assisted with relief mission work, and made personal calls with his pastor. He also accepted a call as temporary pastor of a church in Connecticut. This pastoral experience helped to prepare him for the challenge of other pulpits he would fill during his long ministry.

After seminary he accepted the full-time pastorate of a church in Binghamton, New York, when he was only twenty-three years of age, but, as one writer put it, "his intellectual ability, his growing faith in the Scriptures and his sense of responsibility as an ambassador of God added dignity to his manner and authority to his message."

Throughout his life, Pierson acted upon a conviction to preach the truth without apologizing for it or softening it. He believed "that straight shots are the only ones that can be counted on to hit the mark." During the early years of his ministry, as his uncompromising doctrinal positions became widely known, enemies of the gospel tried to entice him with questions concerning the infallibility of God's Word. Infidels sent him pamphlets and books pointing out "errors and inconsistencies" in the Scriptures. In response, Pierson made a systematic and prayerful study of the Biblical reasons for his beliefs. Finally, he was able to say that the Holy Spirit had given him full assurance of faith. He came to the conclusion "that the Bible is indeed the Word of God and I was prepared to receive it, with all its apparent errors and contradictions, and to wait calmly for their explanation either here or hereafter. . . . I was now prepared to expect some mystery in God's Word, as I saw that otherwise I would be claiming equality with Him. I found that to understand the Bible rightly I must be taught by the Spirit of God and not lean to my own understanding."

After his work at Binghamton, Pierson felt called to a needy work at Waterford, New York. From there, in later years he went on to fill pulpits in Detroit, Indianapolis, and Philadelphia. His last pastoral responsibilities were at the Metropolitan Tabernacle of London, famous because of its pastor, Charles H. Spurgeon. During Spurgeon's illness and immediately after his death, Dr. Pierson provided support and encouragement to the people of the Tabernacle. In every place to which Pierson ministered, he worked to strengthen the congregation doctrinally and to bring in the lost. Church attendance in each place increased markedly, but more importantly, church members attested to tremendous spiritual advancement.

In addition to heavy pastoral responsibilities, Dr. Pierson actively endorsed missions. Throughout his ministry, which was mostly in America,

Dr. Pierson exhibited a zeal for souls, both at home and abroad. In his pastorates, he conducted relief missions in surrounding areas. As opportunities arose, he traveled to Europe, visiting other believers, preaching and conducting campaigns. He encouraged churches to give liberally to the cause of worldwide missions. In his later life, he became a spokesman for missions as editor of the periodical *Missionary Review of the World*. His friendship with George Mueller of England challenged him to live by faith and kept him sympathetic to the needs of orphanages and other mission works. Writing about Dr. Pierson, one biographer observed that "everything else in life [was] subordinated to . . . the doing of God's will and the bringing of men and women to the Saviour's feet."

Along with soulwinning, another great emphasis in Dr. Pierson's ministry was personal holiness. Even as an old man, with an impressive record of dedicated service behind him, he was aware of the need for increasing consecration to the will of God in his life.

With a consuming concern for souls and for righteous living, Dr. Pierson had little inclination to waste time contending for the supremacy of any one denomination. He fellowshiped freely with Wesleyans, Congregationalists, Methodists, Presbyterians, and Baptists. He found spiritual affinity with any Christians whose beliefs and practices were rooted in the fundamentals of the faith. He stated that "no denomination has a monopoly of truth" and that the emphasis in any body of believers should be upon "magnifying the great essentials and yet allowing liberty upon things not essential."

At a Bible conference inaugurated by D. L. Moody at Northfield, Massachusetts, in 1885, Dr. Pierson suggested that a committee be set up to invite fellow evangelicals to "an ecumenical council" for the purpose of expanding missionary efforts around the world. The appointed committee, on which both Pierson and Moody served, was successful in sponsoring the great London Missionary Conference in 1888. There the delegates met for prayer and for powerful messages from the Word of God on the commands to evangelize the world. Reports from missionaries on the field provided impetus to growing missionary consciousness. By 1900 the word "ecumenical," from the Greek word *oikumene* meaning "inhabited earth," began to acquire the connotation it has today—that of uniting diverse religious groups apart from the common ground of doctrinal agreement. Dr. Pierson was saddened when near the end of his life he attended a missions congress and discovered that there were on the platform "those who denied the deity of his Lord or who did not believe in the necessity for faith in His atonement or who unduly exalted humanity to the place of practical deity." He protested that "the message they carried to heathen lands was not the true Gospel." The denominations that had once maintained strong positions on Biblical essentials were now producing unbelievers and apostates. The battle with modern ecumenism had begun.

Dr. Pierson, who during a half century in the ministry wrote over fifty books and innumerable pamphlets, tracts, and magazine articles, is best remembered for his sermons. His son estimated that Dr. Pierson had delivered over thirteen thousand sermons, many of them compiled in book form. These are valuable tools for those who wish to study good preaching and benefit from the renowned preacher's remarkable insight. His style of preaching was predominantly expository, eloquent but always practical. His study of the Scriptures in the original languages yielded treasures which would have remained untouched by casual reading. His sermon illustrations were gleaned from his own rich experiences as well as from his vast knowledge of literature, geography, and science. His question on any subject of his study was "What does the Bible teach?" His emphasis was always upon reaching men's hearts through clear Scriptural principles. Even as a young preacher, he was concerned that "too many modern preachers are not content with using the plain Sword of the Spirit, which in its naked simplicity thrusts deep and cuts quickly. Scholars, instead, forge for themselves swords . . . that are brilliant but have neither point nor edge."

Dr. Pierson's noble bearing and thin, aquiline features gave him a stern appearance. One parishioner described him as "almost too intellectual if it were not for the intense sympathy with his fellow creatures which beams forth from his expressive eyes." His intensity and single-mindedness disconcerted many a parishioner who spoke to him on a city street and received no sign of recognition. His son explained that these apparent slights, which caused his father much regret when he learned of them, were due entirely to the man's unusual powers of concentration. He was quite literally always absorbed in thought on some important matter.

Those who knew him as a preacher knew only one side of him. His wife and seven children knew him as an extremely affectionate, tender man whose life was so godly "as to be well-nigh ascetic." Nonetheless, they would hasten to add that he had a marvelous sense of fun, which surfaced very often in humorous verse composed for special occasions or in notes to friends and family members.

His daily routine was highly disciplined. He devoted much time to prayer and study but always allowed a certain time each evening to relax with his family. The Piersons were a very close family despite the many times when Dr. Pierson was away preaching. Dr. and Mrs. Pierson had the satisfaction of seeing all of their children saved by age fifteen and subsequently engaged in active Christian service.

While practicing self-denial where "treasure on earth" was concerned, Dr. Pierson was lavish with gifts to other people. Nothing delighted him more than to make an anonymous donation to a needy person. Delavan Pierson said that a certain twinkle in his father's eye almost always meant that he had just succeeded in one of his characteristic acts of generosity.

Dr. Pierson spent his life in seemingly tireless service to Christ. Even in his seventies when his health was failing, he refused to alter his busy schedule. He was far more concerned with the soundness of his ministry than with his personal health. Appropriately, Dr. Pierson spent the final months of his life visiting foreign mission fields. Illness shortened his planned itinerary. He died at home in Brooklyn, New York, with his loved ones around him. The service commemorating his homegoing was described thus: "To the eyes of the heavenly spirits that look on this scene this service may be not a funeral but a wedding and the appropriate dress may be not a robe of mourning but a garment of praise."

Suggestions for Further Reading
Delavan Leonard Pierson. *Arthur T. Pierson*. New York: Revell, 1912.
 [Written by his son]

"Plain Billy Sunday"

by Mark Sidwell

The era of the urban evangelists, which began with D. L. Moody, climaxed with the career of Billy Sunday. Perhaps more controversial than Moody—and certainly more sensational—Sunday was a powerful force in American Christianity. He embodied the American ideal of his day—the small-town boy made good and determined to combat the sins of the growing cities. Even more than that, he represented the orthodox Christian solution to society's problems in an era of moral crusades: above all else, save souls.

During a sermon in Des Moines, Iowa, in 1933, seventy-year-old Billy Sunday suffered a heart attack while in the pulpit. As the song leader grasped the staggering evangelist, Sunday pointed to the audience and said urgently, "Don't let them go. They're lost. Give them the invitation. I'd rather die on my feet seeing them come than quit." Although Sunday lived two more years—still preaching all the while— that incident typified the intense, almost consuming drive of the twentieth century's greatest urban evangelist. "I never expect to be an old man," he once told another audience earlier in his career. "I am burning up to do you good and keep you out of hell."

He was born William Ashley Sunday in Iowa in 1862. His father, a soldier in the Union army, never saw Billy. He was in an army camp at the time of his son's birth and died of pneumonia a little more than a month later. Billy's mother was left with three children, a tiny farm, and little with which to make a living. "I am a rube of the rubes," Sunday later said. "I am a graduate of the University of Poverty. I have blacked my boots with stove-blacking, greased my hair with goose grease. I never knew what an undergarment or a nightdress was until I was eighteen years old. I have dried my face and wiped my proboscis on a flour sack towel."

With Mrs. Sunday struggling to make ends meet, Billy bounced around, living sometimes with his mother, sometimes with his grandparents, and for four years in an orphanage in Davenport, Iowa. Sunday might have remained in obscurity except for his athletic skill. Playing for a baseball team in Marshalltown, Iowa, Sunday caught the eye of "Pop" Anson, manager of the Chicago Whitestockings (today's Chicago Cubs). Anson thought that the speedy, agile Sunday would be a solid addition to the Chicago club, and in 1883 he hired Sunday at $60 a month.

Billy Sunday spent eight seasons in the major leagues, compiling a respectable record, primarily as an outfielder, and playing on two pennant-winning teams. More important than his accomplishments on the playing field during this time, however, was God's work of grace in his heart. He met Helen "Nell" Thompson, a devout Presbyterian whose family was not too sure what to make of the scrappy young ball player who was trying to court their daughter. It was not the Thompson family that reached Sunday with the gospel, though. One Sunday afternoon in 1886, while on a drinking binge with his teammates, Sunday heard a group from the Pacific Garden Rescue Mission on the street singing old hymns like those Sunday's mother had sung when he was a boy. Drawn, the ballplayer went to the mission and heard the gospel. He returned several times and finally was converted. (Years later, he showed his gratitude to the mission by giving it the entire $56,000 free-will offering from his Chicago campaign.)

It was a "new" Billy Sunday who married Nell in 1888. He continued to play baseball after his conversion but began to feel burdened to do some sort of Christian work. After much prayer and discussion with his wife, he decided to quit baseball and work for the YMCA. Almost immediately he received a tempting offer to play for the Cincinnati team for $500 a season. He asked Nell what he should do. "There is nothing to consider," she said. "You promised God to quit."

Sunday worked for the YMCA for a few years and then took a position in 1893 as an assistant to Evangelist J. Wilbur Chapman. Sunday worked behind the scenes, going ahead of the rest of the evangelistic team to do the preparation work for each campaign and often speaking to overflow meetings. When Chapman decided to return to the pastorate in 1895, Sunday was at a loss for what to do. Chapman encouraged the young man to become an evangelist, and he even arranged for several churches in Garner, Iowa, to invite Sunday to hold an evangelistic campaign.

Sunday spent several years just learning his trade. He tried at first to imitate the reserved pulpit style of Chapman but found that it did not suit his personality. As he became more comfortable in preaching, Sunday began to let more of his own energetic, boisterous spirit show through, and crowds responded warmly to this sincere if somewhat sensational evangelist. Sunday preached throughout the Midwest in small towns. The evangelist's campaign in Burlington, Iowa, in 1905 was his first "big" revival, and it began a trend. By degrees the Sunday evangelistic team moved into progressively larger cities. In the 1910s Sunday was preaching to huge crowds in the largest cities in the United States, including New York City (one and a half million in attendance), Boston (one and a half million), and Philadelphia (two million).

Sunday's flamboyant style and unusual methods caught the public's eye. Beginning early in his campaigns, for instance, he advertised his meetings, a rare practice in those more conservative days. "Some ministers think it undignified to advertise their services," Sunday said. "It is a good deal more undignified to preach to empty pews, I think." Yet it was his pungent sermons, preached in the vernacular of the man on the street, that won the most attention. Consider the following example from his sermon "The Three Groups":

> I don't expect one of these ossified, petrified, mildewed, dyed-in-the-wool, stamped-on-the-cork, blown-in-the-bottle Presbyterians or Episcopalians to shout "Amen!" but it would do you Methodists good to loosen up. . . . I believe half of the professing Christians amount to nothing as a spiritual force. They go to church, have a kindly regard for religion, but as for having a firm grip on God, . . . and [a] willingness to strike hard, staggering blows against the devil, they are almost failures.

Sunday defended his use of slang to a reporter: "As you see, I use slang scarcely at all in ordinary conversation. I deem it necessary in my work. . . . I want to reach the people so I use the people's language."

Church and city auditoriums soon proved inadequate to hold the growing crowds at Sunday's meetings; so he borrowed an idea that Moody had pioneered—the tabernacle. These large, barnlike structures, each built especially for a campaign, seated thousands on their plain, wooden benches. To deaden noise and settle the dust, the builders poured a layer of sawdust on the ground. Soon newspapers began playing on the idea and described those going down the aisles in response to altar calls as "hitting the sawdust trail."

Exactly how many people "hit the sawdust trail" in Sunday's meetings is uncertain; historians estimate a total of a million over his forty-year career. Interestingly, Sunday's greatest success, in terms of percentage, came in the smaller towns, where up to seventy-five per cent of those who "hit the trail" actually joined a church. And in Jefferson, Iowa, in 1903, the local paper reported that more than half of the unchurched population was converted. However, many who hit the sawdust trail were Christians coming for "reconsecration" (as Sunday called it). The evangelist did not mind. "We know you are in the church," he would tell audiences, "but we want you to get out fully for God." In his Kansas City campaign, for instance, over a third of decisions were for reconsecration.

Sunday's campaigns had their social effects as well. He once said, "The gospel rightly understood and faithfully preached interferes with every form of iniquitous business." This fact was certainly true of the liquor industry. Brewers and distillers considered Billy Sunday one of the men most responsible for establishing nationwide prohibition through passage of the Eighteenth Amendment to the Constitution (1919). In Louisville, Kentucky, in 1914, the bourbon distillers managed to exert enough pressure on church leaders to make them withdraw an invitation to Sunday to hold a campaign there. The evangelist himself was unbending in his hatred of what he called the "damnable, hellish, vile, corrupt, iniquitous liquor business."

The revival trail was not without its unusual side. During a revival in Springfield, Illinois, in 1909, a man leaped from the pews and struck at Sunday twice with a horsewhip, saying, "I have a commission from God to horsewhip you." Sunday leaped from the platform crying, "Well, I have a commission from God to knock the tar out of you, you lobster." One of Sunday's assistants seized the man, but Sunday sprained his ankle from the leap and had to finish the campaign on crutches.

Such incidents, unfortunately, were part of what helped make Billy Sunday's name a household word. Satires of the evangelist abounded. British author P. G. Wodehouse created a preacher named "Jimmy Monday" for one of his "Jeeves and Wooster" stories. Broadway actor George M. Cohan (best remembered today for writing "Over There" and "You're a Grand Old Flag") played a character called "Billy Holliday" in the comedy "Hit the Trail Holliday." Cohan apparently was not too successful in his rendition, however. In reviewing the play, drama critic Heywood Broun wrote, "All in all we believe that Sunday has more of the dramatic instinct than Cohan."

Neither praise nor criticism seemed to make much difference to Billy Sunday. Shortly before his death in 1935, he wrote, "I do not conceal the fact that I am in this world for the purpose of making it easier for people to do right and harder for them to do wrong. . . . I am not a mountebank, I am not . . . a reprint of some one else. I am and always have been plain Billy Sunday trying to do God's will in preaching Jesus and Him crucified and arisen from the dead for our sins."

Suggestions for Further Reading

Lyle W. Dorsett. *Billy Sunday and the Redemption of Urban America.* Grand Rapids: Eerdmans, 1991. [A sympathetic biography based on a thorough study of Sunday's letters and papers]

William G. McLoughlin. *Billy Sunday Was His Real Name.* Chicago: University of Chicago Press, 1955. [A thorough, scholarly study of Sunday's evangelistic methods but somewhat unsympathetic to Sunday himself]

H. C. Morrison and the Holiness Movement

by Timothy Keesee and Mark Sidwell

The Holiness movement brought to American Methodism the fiercest internal conflict in its history. Advocates of Holiness teaching, harking back to John Wesley's little treatise A Plain Account of Christian Perfection *and the works of other early Methodist leaders, sought to call their church back to what they believed were its roots. Among the most powerful preachers of Methodist Holiness was H. C. Morrison. To him—as to others in the movement—Holiness doctrine was in many ways the essence of Christian piety. Morrison said, "Christian perfection is purity of heart, it is perfection of love to God and His creatures; sin is all cleansed away; the character becomes stronger; wisdom increases; the heart is enlarged with love, and the soul grows in all the Christian graces."*

He had the boldness of Cartwright, the zeal of Asbury, and the heart of Wesley. "Long my imprisoned spirit lay"—his preaching echoed Charles Wesley's hymn—"fast bound in sin and nature's night; / Thine eye diffused a quick'ning ray, / I woke, the dungeon flamed with light." H. C. Morrison was aflame—fired by a message of grace and cleansing. For a generation he was one of Methodism's leading figures and among the Holiness movement's most eloquent apologists.

Named for Kentucky's favorite son, Henry Clay Morrison was born in the bluegrass hills near Bedford, Kentucky, on March 10, 1857. Morrison's distinguished name, however, belied a hardscrabble existence during his early years. By the age of four, Morrison had lost both parents, his mother dying when he was two and his father in 1861, the first year of the Civil War. For the divided border state of Kentucky, the early years of the war were grim ones that left a lasting legacy of blood and bitterness.

Faith of Our Fathers: Scenes from American Church History

Poverty and loss, however, were not young Henry's only struggle. As a boy he showed a sensitive spiritual nature. He later recalled, "I was an orphan boy, and I thought that fact would especially appeal to God's compassion. I was surprised as the time passed and instead of peace a heavy load seemed settling down to my heart." Daily he bore the weight of conviction. Even while plowing in the fields, he said, "Satan did certainly walk along the corn rows and seemed to make it appear that he was about the only friend I had."

Morrison at last found the path to peace on the sawdust trail. Converted at a revival meeting at the age of thirteen, he later recounted the experience in full:

> I was wailing aloud, when an old gentleman by the name of Hammer came to me. . . . He stooped down, and in a most tender voice said: "God is not mad at you." The words shot through me. "God loves you," said he, and I ceased to weep; "why, God so loved you that he gave his only Son to die for you," said the good man. His words penetrated me, and it seemed as if my soul, or a voice within me said, "That is so;" and in an instant I was on my feet praising God. My whole heart was aglow with love. I leaped for joy.

As young Henry grew in grace, God led him into the ministry. Licensed to preach by the Methodist Episcopal Church, South, in 1878 and ordained in 1885, Morrison enjoyed success as a circuit rider and a local pastor. As a young minister, he became aware of the growing Holiness movement. He later admitted that he had mistaken notions about Holiness teaching: "I somehow got into my head the notion that they claimed that they had reached a place in the religious life where they could not be tempted, could not commit sin, and had reached a point of such absolute perfection that it was impossible for them to grow in grace. I had gotten the idea of *purity* and *maturity* badly mixed in my mind."

Nonetheless, he studied the issue and became convinced personally of the validity of the idea without immediately experiencing it himself. Instead he claimed that his "second blessing" (i.e., work of the Holy Spirit in subduing the sinful old nature of the Christian) took place during the year 1886-1887. He was pastoring at the time in "the Highlands" near Newport, Kentucky, across the Ohio River from Cincinnati. The event occurred while Morrison was talking with another pastor who was helping him in revival meetings. Morrison describes what happened:

> At that instant the Holy Ghost fell upon me. I fell over on the divan utterly helpless. It seemed as if a great hand had taken hold upon my heart, and was pulling it out of my body. . . . Several moments must have passed, when it seemed to me as if a ball of

fire fell on my face, the sensation of my heart ceased, and I cried out, *"Glory to God!"*. . .

I had received my Pentecost.

It was without doubt the Baptism with the Holy Ghost, and I felt my heart was cleansed from all sin.

After this experience, Morrison did not hesitate to preach the doctrines of Holiness. Those unfamiliar with these teachings may be surprised how often his messages sound like the traditional doctrine of sanctification. "Our *heads* will not be *perfect* in wisdom in this life," Morrison wrote, for example, "but our *hearts may be perfect in love*." He insisted on holiness of life simply as part of salvation: "The plan of redemption does not contemplate the undertaking to make men happy in their sins. It proposes to change men so that sin can give them no pleasure." Nor did the Kentuckian ignore other precious gospel truths in his preaching while stressing this distinctive teaching. The vicarious atonement of Christ, repentance from sin, and justification by faith all took their proper places in his sermons.

Morrison's orthodoxy in general and his Holiness teachings in particular roused some opposition in the Methodist hierarchy. The preacher, for his part, was worried about the Methodist church:

We had a number of men in our Kentucky Methodism who did not lay any special stress on the new birth or the regenerating grace of God. . . . Churches that had been largely filled up with a membership with this idea did not want to be disturbed with "an old-time revival." "Other churches don't have people crying and snivelling at an altar, getting excited, and shouting. Why should we Methodists?" . . .

As for the doctrine of sanctification as taught in the New Testament and interpreted by Mr. Wesley and the early Methodists, it was practically unknown to our people, and strongly opposed by many of our preachers.

This opposition came out into the open when Morrison entered the field of evangelism full-time in 1890. God richly blessed him in this ministry. Crowds flocked to hear his eloquent, earnest sermons in revival services and camp meetings. One meeting in Franklin, Tennessee, was so crowded that the only way he could get into the church was through a window near the pulpit.

Morrison's success, however, served only to provoke his enemies. In 1896 he preached in a camp meeting at a city park in Dublin, Texas. The local Methodist pastor brought charges against him, claiming that the evangelist was preaching in his district without the pastor's permission, an alleged violation of church discipline. Morrison was summarily tried, convicted, and suspended from the ministry. Although Morrison knew that the opposition was motivated more by hatred of his teaching than any real regard for discipline, he refused to be embittered or discouraged. Calmly, he appealed the decision and was acquitted. The denomination declared that according to Methodist regulations, a pastor could forbid someone to preach in his *church,* but not in the *locale* served by the church. Similar attempts to silence Morrison followed, but his opponents finally gave up and left the evangelist to his work.

Despite the conflict with some members of the Methodist hierarchy, Morrison claimed complete loyalty to the Southern Methodist church: "I had no desire for membership in any other denomination. I felt no hint of a call from God to organize a new religious order or movement." Though never a narrow partisan, he proudly rode in Wesley's train with "horse, Holy Bible, and hymn book," preaching the gospel. Conscious of his role as preserver and propagator of historic Methodism, Morrison founded in 1889 the influential *Pentecostal Herald,* which became Methodism's preeminent Holiness publication, intended, says one of Morrison's biographers, *"to defend and fight for all the doctrines, traditions, and customs of Methodism."*

At the age of fifty-three, Morrison added "educator" to his impressive résumé. Tiny Asbury College in Wilmore, Kentucky, had begun in 1890 as a center of Holiness teaching. By 1910, however, financial difficulties threatened the school's existence. The board approached Morrison with a request: Would he take the presidency? Otherwise, they said, they would have to close the school. Morrison accepted, serving his first seven years without salary and using money raised in his evangelistic campaigns to help the school.

For Morrison, Asbury College was to be a "school of the prophets," combining Biblical training with gospel fervor. He expanded the school's ministry, eventually founding Asbury Theological Seminary in 1923. When fellow Methodist evangelist Bob Jones, Sr., was founding his own school, he said to Morrison, "I would appreciate your telling me what to do to build the school successfully. You have had experience in the ministry and also as an educator." Morrision replied, "Well, Bob, I can tell you in a few words. *Keep your chapel platform hot.* No school will die spiritually if you keep your chapel platform hot."

Whether from his own chapel platform, in his publications, or in evangelistic meetings across the country and around the world, Morrison challenged young believers about the joy of the harvest—the call to Christian service. At a revival meeting in Martinsville, Virginia, in 1940, for example, a young man named Frank Washburn suddenly felt the firm hand and piercing look of the old preacher settle upon him. "Son, the Lord bless you when you become a Methodist preacher," Morrison told the startled young man. Morrison's comment became the key to conviction and calling for Washburn, beginning over fifty years of ministry.

The old evangelist would not stop preaching, despite ill health. In March 1942 he held special services in Elizabethton, Tennessee. The eighty-six-year-old preacher suffered an asthma attack, but he attempted to go to the evening service, saying, "If I could get into the pulpit I would have supernatural power . . . to throw this off." When reaching the church, however, he was too ill to enter. The pastor took him into the parsonage, where he died.

Shortly thereafter, a poignant final column from the founding editor of the *Pentecostal Herald* appeared in its pages, prepared with his passing in mind. He noted that "when the readers of the dear old Pentecostal Herald look upon these paragraphs, I shall have passed beyond the veil, and I humbly hope, and have no doubt, shall be worshipping at the feet of my adorable Saviour, our Lord Jesus Christ." Morrison concluded his parting words with a ringing challenge: "My faith in Jesus Christ is without doubt. His power, like His love, is infinite. He is a mighty Christ! His mercies have been over me from my childhood, and now in the evening, I trust Him fully! Blessed be His name forever! Oh, my brethren, . . . be faithful. Be unafraid. Be filled with the Spirit, and pour out to the people a great message, offering them a Christ who is able to save to the uttermost."

Suggestions for Further Reading

H. C. Morrison. *Some Chapters of My Life Story.* Louisville: Pentecostal Publishing Company, 1941.

Delbert R. Rose. *Vital Holiness: A Theology of Christian Experience.* 3rd ed. Minneapolis: Bethany Fellowship, 1975. [The first two chapters (pp. 15-78) survey the background and early history of the Holiness movement.]

Percival A. Wesche. *Crusader Saint: The Life of Henry Clay Morrison.* Wilmore, Ky.: Asbury Theological Seminary, 1963.

Sergeant York: Soldier of Christ

by Mark Sidwell

World War I was a watershed in American history. The conflict brought a crashing end to a century of general world peace and the optimism it engendered. It marked the transformation of the United States from a rural, agricultural society to an urban, industrial one. Alvin C. York, perhaps the greatest individual American hero of the First World War, typified the transition. In some ways a throwback to the simpler ways of rural society, York used the fame he gained by his exploits in France to bring the blessings of progress to his mountain home. Yet he also demonstrated the power of Christ to change and transform a life in any age or circumstance.

Few realize that the greatest of America's military heroes in World War I was also a soldier of Christ. Alvin Cullum York, popularly known as "Sergeant" York, almost single-handedly captured or killed over a hundred Germans during a battle in France's Argonne Forest in 1918. Yet York was no bloodthirsty warmonger, but rather a gentle, quiet man, who had only months before told his commander that it was "against his religion" to kill anyone.

York was born in 1887 in the mountains of northern Tennessee, in the small town of Pall Mall. His mother was a pious woman, his father, a hardworking blacksmith-farmer. York, one of eleven children, grew up working. He developed into one of the finest marksmen in Fentress County, a crack shot who could hit a cross-shaped target carved on a tree dead center from over a hundred feet away. Unfortunately, he also grew into a hard-cursing, hard-drinking, gambling ruffian. One Sunday morning, York used his gun to "carve" his initials into a tree near his mother's church. His mother asked her pastor and friends to pray for her son's salvation.

God answered her prayer in an unusual way. York fell in love with a young girl named Gracie Williams. Gracie, a Christian, let York know in no uncertain terms that she would not have him if he did not mend his ways. Her firmness, added to the testimony and prayers of his mother, brought York to a crossroads. At a revival meeting in a small country church, Alvin York, now under conviction, gave his heart to Christ.

Years later York described the circumstance of his conversion in a complaint about the presentation of that event in a film about his life. (The movie presented his conversion as a result of being struck by lightning.) York said, "That weren't the right down facts of it. You see, I had met Miss Gracie. Miss Gracie said that she wouldn't let me come a-courting until I'd quit my mean drinking, fighting, and card-flipping. So you see I was struck down by the power of love and the Great God Almighty, all together. A bolt of lightning was the nearest to such a thing that Hollywood could think up."

The skeptic may smile at such a "convenient" conversion, "getting religion" in order to win a girl. The testimony of York's life, however, belies such skepticism. A contemporary wrote, "As Mr. Moody used to say, Alvin York was a Christian convert who, when he came from the world, came 'clean out.' . . . To him had come a heavenly vision of the right course of life and, like Paul, he was not disobedient to the heavenly vision. . . . His conversion was so genuine, so thorough, his purpose was so strengthened by the grace of God, that it is the universal testimony that he showed himself to be true to his convictions at all times." However, among the convictions York accepted from his church was pacifism—the total rejection of war and absolute refusal to kill anyone for any reason. On this last point, York fought an arduous spiritual battle.

In 1914 a century of relative peace in Europe ended with the onset of the First World War. By 1917 the United States had been drawn into the conflict. Alvin York received his draft notice and found himself facing a dilemma: Should he follow the dictates of his faith, or fight for his country? His sense of duty would not allow him to shirk his responsibility to his country; so York refused to seek exemption as a conscientious objector. Yet, he understood the sixth commandment—"Thou shalt not kill"—to apply to all situations. York entered the service but later wrote in his diary, "Oh, those were trying times for a boy like me trying to live for God and do his blessed will."

In camp he amazed his superiors with his superb marksmanship; yet York remained uneasy. He told his commander, "Sir, I am doing wrong. Practicing to kill people is against my religion." The commander then placed the young Tennessean in the hands of a major trained to answer religious objections to war. When discussion failed to convince York either way, the army gave him a leave to think it over. After a trying two days back home, he reached the conclusion that duty to country and honor to God did not conflict in time of war. He came back to his family and friends and announced, "I'm goin'."

Faith of Our Fathers: Scenes from American Church History

In October of 1918, a squad of seventeen American soldiers went out to scout enemy positions on Hill No. 223 in the dense Argonne Forest of France. Corporal Alvin York was among the seventeen. The Americans surprised about twenty encamped Germans, including a major, and took them prisoner.

While cautiously leading their prisoners back toward Allied lines, the Americans came upon a large machine gun nest entrenched on the hill. The German guns opened fire, the German prisoners fell immediately to the ground, and the Americans dove for cover. The enemy machine guns killed six Americans and wounded three others.

York, at the front of the American position, found himself isolated from his surviving companions. In the thick underbrush, the other soldiers could not even see the German position. Alone, with only thin shrubbery and the prostrate prisoners between him and the enemy, Corporal York faced the machine gun nest.

York held his rifle and pistol ready. When one of the Germans rose up slightly to view the situation, York fired and the soldier fell back, dead. He watched as one by one, the Germans carefully peered over embankments to get a clear shot at him, and one by one York shot them, using only one bullet for each. The returning German fire hit all around the American but never struck him. Calmly, the Tennessee marksman continued picking off the enemy, continually calling for them to surrender and come down.

Suddenly, six German soldiers broke from the line, charging with fixed bayonets. His rifle clip empty, York raised his automatic pistol and fired, dropping all six still using only one bullet for each. Unnerved at the American's incredible marksmanship, the captive German major told York that he would order the Germans to surrender if only York would stop shooting. York agreed.

The Germans filed out of their positions at the major's orders. The Americans lined up their prisoners two by two. The German major looked at York and the seven other unwounded Americans and asked, "How many men have you?"

"I got a-plenty," replied York.

The Americans marched their prisoners back to Allied lines. The astonished commanders sent back scouts to examine the scene of battle. Amazement spread with the report, for Alvin York had almost single-handedly captured 132 German soldiers, killed 25 others, and silenced 35 machine guns. York, however, credited God and not himself. He wrote in his diary, "I am a witness to the fact God did help me out of that hard battle for the bushes were shot off all around me and I never got a scrach [*sic*]. So you can see that God will be with you if you will only trust Him, and I say He did save me."

Sergeant York: Soldier of Christ

Both civilian and military leaders showered him with honors, including the Congressional Medal of Honor. In presenting York with the Croix de Guerre with Palm (one of France's highest military honors), the supreme commander of the Allied forces in Europe, Marshal Ferdinand Foch, said, "What you did was the greatest thing accomplished by any private soldier of all the armies of Europe." New York gave the homecoming soldier a rousing welcome, and his home state named the new road on which he had labored before the war the "Alvin C. York Memorial Highway" (U.S. 127). The Rotary Club gave him a beautiful, spacious farm in the fertile Wolf River Valley in Fentress County.

York married Gracie Williams in a ceremony performed by the governor of Tennessee himself. When asked countless questions about his adventures in France, York modestly replied, "We know there were miracles, don't we? Well, this was one. It's only way I can figure it."

Sergeant York (he had been promoted after his act of heroism) then retreated from public life. He refused offers for the stage and screen, saying tersely, "This uniform ain't for sale." Instead York turned his attention to that which he believed a serious deficiency among his mountain kindred—education.

Although the veteran's own education came only to about a third grade level, he dreamed of establishing schools in backward areas. In Jamestown, Tennessee, the county seat of Fentress County, York helped establish a grammar and high school as well as an agriculture and trade institute, all named in his honor. York later sought to establish a "school for God," and the little Bible school he founded enrolled over a hundred students at one time. Unfortunately, York's later illnesses forced the closing of the Bible school, but the others remain to this day.

Quietly, Sergeant York tended his farm and took speaking engagements only to raise money to support his schools. Principle remained strong with him, regardless of the situation. Once a tobacco company offered him $500 to speak on a radio program about his war experiences. Although the money would have helped support his schools, York refused to give even tacit endorsement to smoking by appearing on the program. After a long and eventful life, he died in his beloved Tennessee in 1964.

Some men achieve greatness through great deeds done in the sight of the world. Some Christians become heroes of the faith by their steadfast devotion and accomplishments done unto God. Alvin York was a rarity; he was a hero in both senses. Modern society has abandoned the old ideal of a hero—a man of character, courage, principle, and faith. No longer is a man of moral uprightness and religious conviction praised. More often than not, he is mocked. Perhaps Sergeant York is a hero of a past age, but he should be a hero for today, especially for the Christian. "Honest," "humble," and "devout" describe this man. These are simple words, but strong virtues. As a loyal American and soldier of Christ, as a courageous hero and Christian gentleman, Sergeant York stands tall.

Suggestions for Further Reading

Alvin C. York. "The Diary of Sergeant York." In *Great Battles of World War I: On the Land,* edited by Frank C. Platt, pp. 7-51. New York: Signet Books, 1966.

David D. Lee. *Sergeant York: An American Hero.* Lexington: University Press of Kentucky, 1985.

William Jennings Bryan: "He Kept the Faith"

by Douglas Carl Abrams

No figure dominates the period from 1896 to 1925 in American history like William Jennings Bryan. As the leader of the progressive wing of the Democratic party, three times (1896, 1900, 1908) its unsuccessful presidential nominee, and secretary of state under Woodrow Wilson, Bryan placed himself squarely in the center of the major issues of the time. No other public figure in the early twentieth century, with the possible exception of Theodore Roosevelt, enjoyed such sustained and emotional public support. In addition, as this article states, "Bryan, perhaps more than any other major public figure in modern American history, had a clear, public Christian testimony." His was a very diversified career: congressman, lawyer, lecturer, writer, presidential candidate, secretary of state—and Sunday school teacher. He was both statesman and saint.

In the Democratic convention of 1904 in St. Louis, tempers ran hot. Consecutive Republican triumphs in the last two presidential elections had left some party leaders upset and angry with the man whom they felt had led them down to defeat in those campaigns—William Jennings Bryan. Turning their backs on their former standard-bearer, the Democrats nominated conservative jurist Alton Parker to run—vainly— against Theodore Roosevelt in the fall. Forsaken by his party but not cast down in spirit, Bryan addressed the convention with words which aptly characterized both his political career and his religious faith: "You may dispute over whether I have fought a good fight; you may dispute over whether I have finished my course; but you cannot deny that I have kept the faith."

Born in Illinois in 1860 and serving as a lawyer in Nebraska in the 1880s, Bryan early formed the political convictions that put him in the progressive wing of the Democratic party. From his congressional days in the early 1890s until his death in 1925, he made a career of supporting the farmer and the working man against the interests of "big business." His first crusade, which made conservative businessmen his bitter enemies, was that of bimetallism—advocating the coinage of silver in addition to gold in order to increase the money supply. In the 1896 presidential campaign, when Bryan was nominated by both the Democratic and Populist parties, supporters of the gold standard (particularly industrialists and bankers from the East) considered the thirty-six-year-old Nebraskan so radical that they threatened to shut down their businesses if he won. Owners told workers that if they voted for Bryan, they need not report to work the next day. In that campaign Bryan clearly pitted class against class and, to some extent, section against section (the debtor South and West versus the creditor East). From that campaign Bryan earned the "radical" reformist credentials that remained throughout his life, and "Bryanism" never was thought well of in proper conservative circles.

Bryan's position on two other issues, government ownership of the railroads and women's suffrage, strengthened his image as a progressive. He was willing to go even further than the progressive presidents Roosevelt and Wilson. Bryan argued that the best solution for curbing the abuses of the railroad owners, such as exorbitantly high rates, was not just government regulation but government ownership. In a sense, he viewed the railroad as similar to a utility, a service so important to the public that it should not be held in private hands for possible abuse.

Bryan was also an early supporter of women's suffrage. The woman's vote, he believed, would be a vote for reform, for prohibition, and for peace; if men entrusted to women the management of the household and the care of children, they could certainly entrust women with the ballot. In Bryan's view it was a simple matter of justice.

Another aspect of Bryan's public career that sets him apart was his pacifism. Bryan believed that the United States should not resort to war as a part of its foreign policy. He opposed American intervention in world affairs under the McKinley administration and argued that the U.S. had no business engaging in imperialism. As Wilson's secretary of state from 1913 and 1915, he strenuously supported measures to avert World War I and America's entry into it. He resigned from his position when President Wilson protested vigorously to the Germans about their belligerent policies toward neutrals such as the United States. Bryan was afraid that such a strong note from Wilson would bring the nation that much closer to war. Even earlier, Bryan had opposed the lending of funds to the Allies because such a policy would involve the U.S. in the war. However, once President Wilson declared war with congressional approval, Bryan dutifully supported the war effort.

Despite his identification as a progressive in political matters, Bryan, perhaps more than any other major public figure in modern American history, had a clear, public Christian testimony. In his memoirs he gives the following account:

> At the age of fourteen I became a member of the church, as the result of a spiritual awakening that took place in the little town in which I was born. I mention it now because it has had more influence in my life for good than any other experience, and I have been increasingly grateful for the circumstance that led me to take a stand on religion before I left home for college. It was of incalculable value to me during the period of questioning that seems unavoidable in the life of students. The influences of the church, the Sunday school, the prayer meeting, and the YMCA were about me and sustained me until my feet were upon the solid Rock and my faith built upon an enduring foundation. . . . At the age of fourteen, I reached one of the turning points in my life. I attended a revival that was being conducted in a Presbyterian church and was converted.

Throughout his public career, but especially after 1900, Bryan associated himself with Christians and Christian work. He spoke in churches and Bible conferences and in the last few years of his life taught a Sunday school class which usually had about six thousand in attendance. Two of his favorite themes before such Christian groups were prohibition and attacks on evolution. Bryan was one of the major crusaders for the outlawing of liquor and the eventual adoption of the Eighteenth Amendment. After World War I Bryan also vehemently attacked the teaching of evolution in public schools and colleges; he saw evolution as a direct threat to Christian civilization and an assault on the Bible. Bryan supported efforts in various states to pass anti-evolution laws. Also in his later years he served as an elder in the Presbyterian church and at the time of his death was vice-moderator of the denomination. Bryan willingly associated himself with the leading fundamentalists of the day, such as Billy Sunday.

How does one reconcile Bryan's progressive political views with his staunchly fundamentalist religious views? For Bryan there was no contradiction; it was all part of the reform movement. Evolution, liquor, war, crooked businessmen, and corrupt monopolies all represented aspects of American society that the Christian must fight and eliminate. Bryan enjoyed the support of two constituencies—political progressives and religious conservatives—and he clearly associated with both throughout his career. Bryan was not a progressive in the late 1890s and then a fundamentalist in the early 1920s; he was both at the same time. One must remember that the emphasis of his day was different from what it is today. The enemy for most Americans at the turn of the century was big business; the dangers of "big government" did not become so evident until after the New Deal of Franklin Roosevelt.

William Jennings Bryan became a hero to fundamentalists particularly through his efforts at the Scopes trial in Dayton, Tennessee. When Tennessee passed a law banning the teaching of evolution in its schools, some leaders of Dayton hoped to put their town on the map by coaxing a high school teacher, John T. Scopes, to challenge the law. The result was a media event as national attention focused on the town for the summer of 1925. Bryan helped the prosecution and served as an expert witness on the Bible. Clarence Darrow, expert trial lawyer and agnostic, defended Scopes. Although Bryan was hesitant to testify, he declared to the court, "I want the Christian world to know that any atheist, agnostic, unbeliever, can question me any time as to my belief in God, and I will answer him." Unfortunately, Bryan was no Bible scholar, and he did not make the best case for his cause. Scopes was convicted, but Bryan and the antievolutionists lost the publicity battle. There was, however, no question about his courage. Following his death only days after the Scopes trial, Bryan was buried in Arlington National Cemetery. On his tomb was an epitaph simple and powerful: "He Kept the Faith."

Suggestions for Further Reading

Lawrence W. Levine. *Defender of the Faith, William Jennings Bryan: The Last Decade.* New York: Oxford University Press, 1965.

C. Allyn Russell. "William Jennings Bryan, Statesman-Fundamentalist," Chapter 7 in *Voices of American Fundamentalism.* Philadelphia: Westminster Press, 1976, pp. 162-89. [A good though mildly critical discussion of Bryan as a fundamentalist]

J. Gresham Machen and the Fundamentalist Movement

by Mark Sidwell

> *Both the Holiness movement and fundamentalism opposed the spread of religious liberalism. A chief difference between the movements was that Holiness Christians tended to emphasize correct* behavior *whereas fundamentalism tended to emphasize correct* doctrine. *No fundamentalist embodied this emphasis on doctrine more than its greatest scholar, J. Gresham Machen.*

It would seem that J. Gresham Machen participated in every kind of struggle that characterized the fundamentalist-modernist controversy. He was a leading force in the ultimately vain efforts to preserve the Presbyterian Church in the U.S.A. and later Princeton Seminary from liberal domination. He resisted the inroads of modernism on the mission field and for his efforts was eventually expelled by his own denomination. Afterwards, in order to help defend "the faith which was once delivered unto the saints" (Jude 3), he helped found both an orthodox seminary and a denomination. Yet, ironically, he remained uneasy with the fundamentalist label and feared for the movement's future.

Born in Maryland in 1881, John Gresham Machen was from an upper-middle class family, graced with a touch of Southern gentility. A brilliant student, he graduated from Johns Hopkins University in 1901. But Machen was also a devout Christian. He felt drawn to the Christian ministry but was so aware of his own shortcomings that he felt unworthy of the office. Machen told to his family that a Presbyterian minister counseled him to attend Princeton Theological Seminary, explaining— Machen wrote—"that *if* I want to leave after a year, it will do me no harm." He entered Princeton in 1902 and, aside from brief periods of study in Europe, remained there as a student or teacher for well over twenty-five years. His hesitancy in entering the ministry finally overcome, he was ordained in 1914 and became a powerful preacher of the Word.

Machen joined the faculty of Princeton Seminary in 1906, teaching in the field of New Testament, especially Greek. (His *New Testament Greek for Beginners,* published in 1923, became a standard text in many schools and has gone through over forty printings.) Princeton was still in its glory days when Machen came. Some of the most brilliant theologians of orthodoxy had served there—Archibald Alexander, Charles Hodge, and Benjamin B. Warfield, to name just a few. Machen soon proved himself a worthy heir of Princeton. His teaching was clear and instructive, and his writings showed the same careful scholarship and love of Biblical truth that had characterized the earlier Princetonians. Among Machen's outstanding works were *The Origin of Paul's Religion* (1927) and his masterpiece, *The Virgin Birth of Christ* (1930), both of which were scholarly defenses of Christian truth in the face of modernist attack.

Perhaps his most famous work, though, was one bound up in the fundamentalist-modernist controversy. In *Christianity and Liberalism* (1923), Machen set forth the irrepressible conflict between Christianity and modernism—two entirely different religions in Machen's view. The struggle within the denominations was not a clash of differing interpretations of the Christian faith, he said; "it is really an issue between Christianity . . . on the one side, and a naturalistic negation of all Christianity on the other." Later in the book he stated even more bluntly, "The greatest menace to the Christian Church to-day comes not from the enemies outside, but from the enemies within; it comes from the presence within the Church of a type of faith and practice that is anti-Christian to the core."

In the face of growing liberalism, the Presbyterian Church in the U.S.A. had three times (1910, 1916, 1923) stated that candidates for the ministry must affirm their belief in essential Christian doctrines, such as Christ's virgin birth, His vicarious atonement, and His bodily resurrection. In 1923, however, a group of nearly 150 Presbyterian clergy headquartered in Auburn, New York, protested that such statements of faith should not be required for ordination. This "Auburn Affirmation" touched off a prolonged battle over whether the PCUSA was to maintain its commitment to orthodox Christianity.

Machen, of course, supported the fundamentalist party. He was, to be honest, in some ways atypical of fundamentalism. He actually cared little for the term *fundamentalist,* saying, "It seems to suggest that we are adherents of some strange new sect, whereas in point of fact we are conscious simply of maintaining the historic Christian faith and of moving in the great central current of Christian life." In addition, he disliked the tendency of some fundamentalists to reduce the Christian faith to a handful of essential doctrines, and he regretted the anti-intellectualism that many fundamentalists displayed. Yet he stated in 1926, "Do you suppose that I do not regret my being called . . . a 'Fundamentalist'? Most certainly I do. But in the presence of a great common foe, I have little time to be attacking my brethren who stand with me in defense of the Word of God.'' And in 1927 he said in a letter that ''if the disjunction is between 'Fundamentalism' and 'Modernism,' then I am willing to call myself a Fundamentalist of the most pronounced type.''

Eventually, however, a coalition of liberals and conservatives who desired to preserve denominational unity moved the PCUSA from its orthodox doctrinal requirements for ministers. Now firmly in control of the denominational machinery, the liberals pushed through in 1929 a re-organization of the board of the PCUSA's most conservative seminary— Princeton. Unwilling to serve under a liberal-dominated board, Machen, several other Princeton faculty members, and a number of students left that school to form Westminster Theological Seminary in 1929.

The battle in the Presbyterian church was not over yet. Dismayed by the number of modernists serving on the mission field, Machen joined other conservatives in forming the Independent Board for Presbyterian Foreign Missions in 1933. Accusing Machen of causing schism by establishing a board not approved by the church, the denomination tried him and suspended him from the ministry in 1935. Machen was not even allowed to defend himself at his hearing.

In *Christianity and Liberalism* Machen had written, ''If the liberal party . . . really obtains control of the Church, evangelical Christians must be prepared to withdraw no matter what it costs. Our Lord has died for us, and surely we must not deny Him for favor of men.'' Showing that these words were not an empty boast, Machen rejected all efforts to reconcile him to a church which he now feared was lost to the cause of Christ. Instead, he eagerly led in 1935 in the formation of what eventually became known as Orthodox Presbyterian Church. It was while preaching in some of the struggling churches of this new denomi-nation in Bismarck, North Dakota, that he contracted pneumonia in 1937 and died.

In 1925, in the midst of the Presbyerian conflict, Machen wrote, ''Christian doctrine, I hold, is not merely connected with the gospel, but it is identical with the gospel, and if I did not preach it at all times, and especially in those places where it subjects me to personal abuse, I should regard myself as guilty of sheer unfaithfulness to Christ.'' By this standard, not even Machen's enemies could ever charge that he was ever in any way ''guilty'' of anything except unswerving faithfulness to Jesus Christ.

Suggestions for Further Reading

J. Gresham Machen. *Christianity and Liberalism.* 1923. Reprint. Grand Rapids: Eerdmans, 1981.

Henry W. Coray. *J. Gresham Machen, A Silhouette.* Grand Rapids: Kregel, 1981.

Faith of Our Fathers: Scenes from American Church History

C. Allyn Russell. "J. Gresham Machen, Scholarly Fundamentalist," Chapter 6 in *Voices of American Fundamentalism.* Philadelphia: Westminster Press, 1976, pp. 135-61. [A good sketch but the author is critical in his conclusions]

Ned B. Stonehouse. *J. Gresham Machen: A Biographical Memoir.* Grand Rapids: Eerdmans, 1954.

Ford Porter, Gentle Fundamentalist

by Dan Olinger

Fundamentalists are perhaps best known for their fighting spirit, which sometimes finds its objects beyond the enemies of the faith. This characterization, however, is often inaccurate; and one of the best illustrations of the fundamentalist's doctrinal stead- fastness combined with a gentle and humble spirit was Ford Por- ter. His life is instructional not only for its combination of these elements but also for the reason he was that way. He proved that one need not be contentious in order to "contend for the faith."

Ford Porter was born in a farmhouse in Ottawa County, Michigan, on February 5, 1893—the fifty-sixth birthday of Dwight L. Moody. His parents were both godly Christians, and while he was still young the family initiated, at his mother's suggestion, a regular time of family devotions. The practice continued until the children were grown, and Porter recognized early the importance of the Scriptures and prayer in the lives of his parents.

At the age of eleven, during a revival meeting in his home church in Sparta, Michigan, young Porter went forward to confess his sin and acknowledge his need of a Saviour. His father died shortly thereafter, however, and Porter soon drifted away from the godly influence of his mother, though not from the reach of her prayers. In 1916, after eight years of rebellion, Porter attended a citywide evangelistic campaign in Evansville, Indiana, held by Henry Stough. At the end of a sermon on fathers and sons, Porter, convicted by the Holy Spirit and recognizing his rebellion against the memory of his earthly father as well as against the mercy of his heavenly Father, again went forward and asked for- giveness for his sins.

Porter did not enter immediately into full-time Christian work. He was at the time supervisor of a factory shipping department, and he began to share with his workers the testimony of the grace of God in his life. At the employees' request, he instituted a regular weekly meet- ing in the factory for a time of testimony and Bible study. The meetings continued for over three years.

During this time Porter came under the spiritual tutelage of Ernest Reveal, founder and director of the Evansville Rescue Mission. Reveal encouraged the spiritual neophyte to get involved in more formal evangelistic outreaches, including evangelistic campaigns and tract distribution. This exposure to evangelism through the inexpensive written word was to have a profound impact on the outcome of Porter's ministry.

On February 5, 1918, Porter's twenty-fifth birthday, he began a practice that would characterize and direct the rest of his life. He ascended to the unheated attic of his house early in the morning and knelt next to the warmth of the chimney, where he spent the next hour in prayer. He was later, and often, to observe that "prayer is God's means for carrying on His work down here on this earth." It was perhaps the role of prayer in his life that kept him gentle and humble through the divisive conflicts in which he unflinchingly stood.

On the first two days of his regular prayer, he requested two things: a ministry that would encircle the world and continue after his death, and one that would help him train young people for Christian service. The second prayer was answered almost immediately.

Porter's home church was affiliated with the Northern Baptist Convention, and the pastor invited Porter to take over the leadership of the church's Baptist Young People's Union (B.Y.P.U.). He was soon elected president of the regional B.Y.P.U. and then to the national board and to the office of national recording secretary. His travels in connection with those offices, however, brought to his attention a troubling trend in the Northern Baptist Convention: the encroachment of liberalism. In 1928, the year he was asked to accept nomination to the presidency of the B.Y.P.U., he broke his association with the organization, thereby setting the stage for a much more intense battle to follow.

Porter took his first pastorate in 1922, an outreach church founded by the Evansville Rescue Mission. Four years later he accepted a call to the First Baptist Church of Princeton, Indiana, which was to be the site of a battle that would place him and his flock in direct conflict with the increasingly liberal denominational hierarchy.

In 1938, twelve years after Porter accepted the pastorate of the church, the congregation voted by a substantial majority (92 to 18) to withdraw from the Convention, based on several evidences of liberalism: the Convention's refusal in 1922 to adopt the New Hampshire Statement of Faith; its decision in 1925 not to require a doctrinal test of its missionary candidates; its election to the presidency of the Convention a man who had questioned in print the atoning value of the crucifixion; and its giving of Convention funds to the Federal Council of Churches and other organizations that denied, among other things, the value of the blood of Christ.

On the night of the vote, the eighteen defeated members met with denominational leaders to plan to present themselves as the recognized church body. To prevent the minority from establishing legal ownership of the church properties by default, the church majority obtained a court restraining order against the minority until the issue of ownership and legal identity could be settled.

The issue in the court case was whether the majority could legally withdraw from the Convention, and thus whether the Convention was justified in recognizing the minority, which had voted to remain in the Convention, as the official church. One point in the testimony revealed the Convention's duplicity. T. J. Parsons, Executive Secretary of the Indiana Baptist Convention, was being cross-examined by the counsel for the plaintiffs (the majority, who had voted to withdraw):

Q. Doctor Parsons, you answered Mr. Trippet on direct examination that in the event the majority of a church should vote to withdraw fellowship from the . . . Northern Baptist Convention and a minority opposed that action, they would consider the minority the true church.

A. Yes, sir.

Q. Now in the event that should be reversed, and the minority would vote to withdraw fellowship and the majority should be opposed to withdraw fellowship, who would you consider the true church then?

A. The majority that remained with the denomination.

Q. In other words, whichever retained fellowship would be the true church.

A. Sure.

. . .

Q. How would a church ever break fellowship with the Northern Baptist Convention?

. . .

A. If a church unanimously voted to withdraw from the convention, then the whole body of that church goes out.

Q. And if one single member of that church voted against withdrawing from the convention, that one person would be the true church, in your judgment?

A. That is not a proper question, in my estimation.

Q. The court rules on whether a question is proper or not. . . .

A. We would recognize that one member and defend his rights.

Q. And he would be the church?

A. Yes, because he did not go out.

Porter later commented, "It was such ridiculous testimony as this that . . . helped the judge to decide as he did without our having to put a single witness on the stand.'' When the Convention closed its presentation, the judge found immediately in favor of the majority, and his decision was upheld on appeal. Porter shared the ''secret'' of the church's victory:

> It is doubtful if there has been any single matter come before all of the churches of like faith and order that has given occasion for more prayer and supplication than this particular matter. This local church has spent weeks in prayer, someone taking each hour of the day and night for seven days in succession, and also there have been many single days with someone waiting upon the Lord each hour throughout the day and night, and some fasting. . . . During the different trials, there was a peculiar consciousness of the presence of the Holy Spirit. At times when important decisions were to be made, many testified of having been moved to tears just because of the presence of the Lord.

In 1940 Porter accepted a call to another church, Berean Missionary Baptist in Indianapolis. After seven years there, he saw the Lord open the door to the answer to his first prayer in that cold attic nearly thirty years before. Berean began expanding its ministry to include multiple outreaches: a radio ministry, children's Bible crusades, a camp, an institute to train Vacation Bible School workers, a film department, and a Bible institute. But the outreach for which Porter is best remembered is the writing and producing of a tract called ''God's Simple Plan of Salvation,'' which he had first written in 1933. Although he died in 1976, through the tract he continues to speak to sinners of the saving grace of God. By the 1990s, over 460 *million* copies of ''God's Simple Plan of Salvation'' had been printed in 104 different languages.

This little tract is peculiarly appropriate as a symbol of Porter's life. For despite his willingness to stand against false teaching and to call apostates what they were, he was most centrally a gentle and humble man. While other pastors labored to build great monuments to themselves, he said repeatedly, ''Rather than compromise my position, I will die in obscurity.'' While others are remembered through great buildings and organizations, Porter is remembered for a little one-sheet, two-color tract, aptly named ''God's Simple Plan of Salvation.'' Through this one message, conversationally presenting to the sinner the great love of God, this gentle fundamentalist has proved God faithful to His word and has left an undying legacy.

Suggestions for Further Reading

Ford Porter. *We Still Have an Autonomous Church*. Princeton, Ind.: Standard Printing Co., n.d.

Herbert Lockyer. *The Berean Miracle*. Indianapolis: Berean Gospel Distributors, 1963.

About the Contributors

Mark Sidwell (general editor) has a Ph.D. in church history from Bob Jones University and works as an author and editor at Bob Jones University Press. He has written several journal articles and is the co-author of *United States History for Christian Schools* (2nd ed.).

Douglas Carl Abrams has a Ph.D. in history from the University of Maryland. He teaches graduate and undergraduate courses in American history and political science at Bob Jones University and also leads a summer mission team to Kenya. He is the author of numerous journal articles and has contributed articles to *Political Parties and Elections in the United States: An Encyclopedia*. He has finished a book on North Carolina and the New Deal and is currently working on a social history of fundamentalism during the twenties and thirties.

David O. Beale has a Ph.D. in church history from Bob Jones University. He is a teacher in the School of Religion at Bob Jones University and a professor of church history in Bob Jones Seminary and Division of Graduate Studies. He is the author of *In Pursuit of Purity: American Fundamentalism Since 1850; SBC: House on the Sand?;* and *A Pictorial History of Our English Bible*. He takes a particular interest in colonial American church history. Research for the article on Francis Makemie (pp. 28-31) was provided by Mrs. Terry Kane, Dr. Beale's mother.

Carolyn P. Cooper is a member of the editorial department at Bob Jones University Press.

Gene Elliott has a Ph.D. in library science from Florida State University and formerly served as Director of the Library at Bob Jones University. He is currently Director of Library Services at Greenville Technical College in Greenville, South Carolina.

Rebecca Lunceford Foster formerly served as Editorial Assistant of *FAITH for the Family* magazine and was a regular contributor to that periodical. She now resides in Raytown, Missouri.

Karen Guffey was formerly a member of the Spanish faculty at Bob Jones University and served as Editorial Assistant for *FAITH for the Family* magazine. She has also taught Spanish and English at Maranatha Baptist Bible College and currently resides in Lexington, Kentucky, where she is working on a Ph.D. in Spanish.

Christa G. Habegger is a member of the voice faculty at Bob Jones University and author of *Saints and Non-Saints,* a collection of articles on real and fictional characters in church history.

Sandra Harber is a free-lance writer.

Craig Jennings has a Ph.D. in church history from Bob Jones University and is currently professor of church history at the Association Free Lutheran Bible School and Seminary in Minneapolis.

Bob Jones is the Chancellor and former President of Bob Jones University. He is a noted preacher, Shakespearean actor, and art expert. He has written many books, including the novels *Wine of Morning* and *Daniel of Babylon* and nonfiction works such as *How to Improve Your Preaching* and *Cornbread and Caviar.*

Timothy Keesee has an Ed.D. from Bob Jones University and serves there as head of the Public Liaison Office. He has written *American Government for Christian Schools* and *The Political Christian* and co-authored *United States History for Christian Schools* (2nd ed.).

Rachel C. Larson is a history instructor at Bob Jones Academy and author of the junior high textbook *The American Republic for Christian Schools.* She is currently a Ph.D. candidate in American history at Emory University.

Mark Minnick has a Ph.D. in New Testament from Bob Jones University. He is a member of the Bible faculty at the University and pastor of the Mt. Calvary Baptist Church in Greenville, South Carolina.

George Mulfinger, Jr., until his death in 1987, was a member of the science faculty at Bob Jones University. He wrote numerous articles and pamphlets, including *The Flood and the Fossils* and *How Did the Earth Get Here?* He also edited the anthology *Design and Origins in Astronomy* and co-authored the first textbook published by Bob Jones University Press, *Physical Science for Christian Schools* (1974).

Dan Olinger has a Ph.D. in theology from Bob Jones University and is Product Development Coordinator, Secondary Level, at Bob Jones University Press. He has written numerous articles and the booklets *Homosexuality* and *British Israelism.*

Edward M. Panosian has a Ph.D. in church history from Bob Jones University. He is the Chairman of the Division of Social Science at Bob Jones University and is a professor of church history in Bob Jones Seminary and Division of Graduate Studies. He is the author of numerous articles and the booklet *The World Council of Churches.*

Richard Rupp formerly served as Director of Extension and Ministerial Training at Bob Jones University and is currently Missions Counselor for Gospel Fellowship Association Missions.

Dayton Walker is a real estate agent and member of the city council in Greenville, South Carolina.

Susan Lindner Zimmerman formerly served as an editor and writer for *FAITH for the Family* magazine. A 1974 graduate of Bob Jones University, she currently resides in Wheaton, Illinois, where she is a wife, mother, and free-lance business and technical copywriter.

Index